On the Horizon

COVER
ILLUSTRATOR

SPOTLIGHT

ROBERT HYNES

❖ When Robert Hynes was in third grade, he liked playing with his friends—and drawing. "Actually, I had friends who loved to draw. So we would come in from baseball and draw. We had 'draw-ins'!" His career in art began when he won a competition to create the bicentennial murals for the Smithsonian Institution.

❖ The snow animals on the cover of this book first took form in Mr. Hynes's lively imagination. He wanted his moonlit snowscape to be both magical and real.

Acknowledgments appear on pages 350–351, which constitute an extension of this copyright page.

© 1993 Silver Burdett Ginn Inc.
Cover art © 1993 by Robert Hynes.

ISBN 0–663–54657–5

2 3 4 5 6 7 8 9 10 RRD 98 97 96 95 94 93

New Dimensions
IN THE
WORLD OF READING

On the Horizon

P R O G R A M   A U T H O R S

James F. Baumann   Roselmina Indrisano   P. David Pearson
Theodore Clymer   Dale D. Johnson   Taffy E. Raphael
Carl Grant   Connie Juel   Marian Davies Toth
Elfrieda H. Hiebert   Jeanne R. Paratore   Richard L. Venezky

SILVER BURDETT GINN

NEEDHAM, MA   MORRISTOWN, NJ

ATLANTA, GA   DALLAS, TX   DEERFIELD, IL   MENLO PARK, CA

Unit 1 Theme

One of a Kind

Unit 2 Theme

Gather 'Round

Unit 3 Theme

Working It Out

Unit 4 Theme

Weather or Not

10

One of a Kind

Everyone is special in some way.

What makes some people special to read about?

COCHITI STORYTELLERS, *Pueblo pottery by Rita Lewis, Helen Cordero, Ada Suina, American, 1964*

13

Theme Books for
One of a Kind

Do you know a special, one-of-a-kind person? Even when someone seems ordinary, look more closely. Everyone is unique in some special way.

❖ In **Perfect Crane** by Anne Laurin, lonely Gami is filled with joy when he brings an origami crane to life. But one day the crane says that he must leave. How will Gami manage without his best friend?

Of all the night animals, Coyote is the Moon's favorite in ***The Moon, the Sun, and the Coyote*** by Judith Cole. Even when the Moon makes Coyote a great and handsome hunter, he is not satisfied. What will the Moon do when Coyote begs her to make him even more special?

More Books to Enjoy

Who's That Girl with the Gun?
    by Robert Quackenbush
Beats Me, Claude by Joan Lowery Nixon
Ramona the Brave by Beverly Cleary
Louis Braille by Margaret Davidson

The Big Orange SPLOT

written and illustrated by
Daniel Manus Pinkwater

Mr. Plumbean lived on a street where all the houses were the same.

He liked it that way. So did everybody else on Mr. Plumbean's street. "This is a neat street," they would say. Then one day . . .

A sea gull flew over Mr. Plumbean's house. He was carrying a can of bright orange paint. (No one knows why.) And he dropped the can (no one knows why) right over Mr. Plumbean's house.

It made a big orange splot on Mr. Plumbean's house.

"Ooooh! Too bad!" everybody said. "Mr. Plumbean will have to paint his house again."

16

"I suppose I will," said Mr. Plumbean. But he didn't paint his house right away. He looked at the big orange splot for a long time; then he went about his business.

The neighbors got tired of seeing that big orange splot. Someone said, "Mr. Plumbean, we wish you'd get around to painting your house."

"O.K.," said Mr. Plumbean.

He got some blue paint and some white paint, and that night he got busy. He painted at night because it was cooler.

When the paint was gone, the roof was blue. The walls were white. And the big orange splot was still there.

Then he got some more paint. He got red paint, yellow paint, green paint, and purple paint.

In the morning the other people on the street came out of their houses. Their houses were all the same. But Mr. Plumbean's house was like a rainbow. It was like a jungle. It was like an explosion.

There was the big orange splot. And there were little orange splots. There were stripes. There were pictures of elephants and lions and pretty girls and steam shovels.

The people said, "Plumbean has popped his cork, flipped his wig, blown his stack, and dropped his stopper." They went away muttering.

That day Mr. Plumbean bought carpenter's tools. That night he built a tower on top of his roof, and he painted a clock on the tower.

The next day the people said, "Plumbean has gushed his mush, lost his marbles, and slipped his hawser." They decided they would pretend not to notice.

That very night Mr. Plumbean got a truck full of green things. He planted palm trees, baobabs, thorn bushes, onions, and frangipani. In the morning he bought a hammock and an alligator.

When the other people came out of their houses, they saw Mr. Plumbean swinging in a hammock between two palm trees. They saw an alligator lying in the grass. Mr. Plumbean was drinking lemonade.

"Plumbean has gone too far!"

"This used to be a neat street!"

"Plumbean, what have you done to your house?" the people shouted.

"My house is me and I am it. My house is where I like to be and it looks like all my dreams," Mr. Plumbean said.

The people went away. They asked the man who lived next door to Mr. Plumbean to go and have a talk with him. "Tell him that we all liked it here before he changed his house. Tell him that his house has to be the same as ours so we can have a neat street."

The man went to see Mr. Plumbean that evening. They sat under the palm trees drinking lemonade and talking all night long.

Early the next morning the man went out to get lumber and rope and nails and paint. When the people came out of their houses they saw a

red and yellow ship next door to the house of Mr. Plumbean.

"What have you done to your house?" they shouted at the man.

"My house is me and I am it. My house is where I like to be and it looks like all my dreams," said the man, who had always loved ships.

"He's just like Plumbean!" the people said. "He's got bees in his bonnet, bats in his belfry, and knots in his noodle!"

Then, one by one, they went to see Mr. Plumbean, late at night. They would sit under the palm trees and drink lemonade and talk about their dreams—and whenever anybody visited Mr. Plumbean's house, the very next day that person would set about changing his own house to fit his dreams.

Whenever a stranger came to the street of Mr. Plumbean and his neighbors, the stranger would say, "This is not a neat street."

Then all the people would say, "Our street is us and we are it. Our street is where we like it to be, and it looks like all our dreams."

Reader's Response ∿ Which would you like better, the neat street or the new street? Why?

Library Link ∿ *If you would like to read more books by Daniel Manus Pinkwater, look in the library for* Blue Moose, Fat Men from Space, *and* Roger's Umbrella.

Just for LAUGHS

Are writers of humorous stories funny in person? Judge for yourself!

Daniel Manus Pinkwater claims to own two rhinoceroses and "a collection of false noses that may be the largest and most complete" in the world.

He once invented a secretary named Wally Wanamopo who sent a letter to a publisher stating that Mr. Pinkwater had been captured by an alien spaceship, adding, "It is my hope that the beings will return Mr. Pinkwater. There is reason to believe this will happen—numerous accounts exist of people who have been captured by 'space men' and have been subsequently returned. I think this is likely to be the case with my employer, particularly if the space beings have a limited supply of food."

Maybe the aliens kept Mr. Pinkwater on board...just for laughs!

Miss Rumphius

written and illustrated
by Barbara Cooney

The Lupine Lady lives in a small house overlooking the sea. In between the rocks around her house grow blue and purple and rose-colored flowers. The Lupine Lady is little and old. But she has not always been that way. I know. She is my great-aunt, and she told me so.

Once upon a time she was a little girl named Alice, who lived in a city by the sea. From the front stoop she could see the wharves and the bristling masts of tall ships. Many years ago her grandfather had come to America on a large sailing ship.

Now he worked in the shop at the bottom of the
house, making figureheads for the prows of ships,
and carving Indians out of wood to put in front of
cigar stores. For Alice's grandfather was an artist. He
painted pictures, too, of sailing ships and places
across the sea. When he was very busy, Alice helped
him put in the skies.

23

In the evening, Alice sat on her grandfather's knee and listened to his stories of faraway places. When he had finished, Alice would say, "When I grow up, I too will go to faraway places, and when I grow old, I too will live beside the sea."

"That is all very well, little Alice," said her grandfather, "but there is a third thing you must do."

"What is that?" asked Alice.

"You must do something to make the world more beautiful," said her grandfather.

"All right," said Alice. But she did not know what that could be.

In the meantime, Alice got up and washed her face and ate porridge for breakfast. She went to school and came home and did her homework.

And pretty soon she was grown up.

Then my Great-aunt Alice set out to do the three things she had told her grandfather she was going to do. She left home and went to live in another city far from the sea and the salt air. There she worked in a library, dusting books and keeping them from getting mixed up, and helping people find the ones they wanted. Some of the books told her about faraway places.

People called her Miss Rumphius now.

Sometimes she went to the conservatory in the middle of the park. When she stepped inside on a wintry day, the warm moist air wrapped itself around her, and the sweet smell of jasmine filled her nose.

"This is almost like a tropical isle," said Miss Rumphius. "But not quite."

So Miss Rumphius went to a real tropical island, where people kept cockatoos and monkeys as pets. She walked on long beaches, picking up beautiful shells. One day she met the Bapa Raja, king of a fishing village.

"You must be tired," he said. "Come into my house and rest."

So Miss Rumphius went in and met the Bapa Raja's wife. The Bapa Raja himself fetched a green coconut and cut a slice off the top so that Miss Rumphius could drink the coconut water inside. Before she left, the Bapa Raja gave her a beautiful mother-of-pearl shell on which he had painted a bird of paradise and the words, "You will always remain in my heart."

"You will always remain in mine too," said Miss Rumphius.

My great-aunt Miss Alice Rumphius climbed tall mountains where the snow never melted. She went through jungles and across deserts. She saw lions playing and kangaroos jumping. And everywhere she made friends she would never forget. Finally she came to the Land of the Lotus-Eaters, and there, getting off a camel, she hurt her back.

"What a foolish thing to do," said Miss Rumphius. "Well, I have certainly seen faraway places. Maybe it is time to find my place by the sea."

And it was, and she did.

From the porch of her new house, Miss Rumphius watched the sun come up; she watched it cross the heavens and sparkle on the water; and she saw it set in glory in the evening. She started a little garden among the rocks that surrounded her house, and she planted a few flower seeds in the stony ground. Miss Rumphius was *almost* perfectly happy.

"But there is still one more thing I have to do," she said. "I have to do something to make the world more beautiful."

But what? "The world already is pretty nice," she thought, looking out over the ocean.

The next spring Miss Rumphius was not very well. Her back was bothering her again, and she had to stay in bed most of the time.

The flowers she had planted the summer before had come up and bloomed in spite of the stony ground. She could see them from her bedroom window, blue and purple and rose-colored.

"Lupines," said Miss Rumphius with satisfaction. "I have always loved lupines the best. I wish I could plant more seeds this summer so that I could have still more flowers next year."

But she was not able to.

After a hard winter spring came. Miss Rumphius was feeling much better. Now she could take walks again. One afternoon she started to go up and over the hill, where she had not been in a long time.

"I don't believe my eyes!" she cried when she got to the top. For there on the other side of the hill was a large patch of blue and purple and rose-colored lupines!

"It was the wind," she said as she knelt in delight. "It was the wind that brought the seeds from my garden here! And the birds must have helped!"

Then Miss Rumphius had a wonderful idea!

She hurried home and got out her seed catalogues. She sent off to the very best seed house for five bushels of lupine seed.

All that summer Miss Rumphius, her pockets full of seeds, wandered over fields and headlands, sowing lupines. She scattered seeds along the highways and down the country lanes. She flung handfuls of them around the schoolhouse and back of the church. She tossed them into hollows and along stone walls.

Her back didn't hurt her any more at all.

Now some people called her That Crazy Old Lady.

The next spring there were lupines everywhere. Fields and hillsides were covered with blue and purple and rose-colored flowers. They bloomed along the highways and down the lanes. Bright patches lay around the schoolhouse and back of the church.

Down in the hollows and along the stone walls grew the beautiful flowers.

Miss Rumphius had done the third, the most difficult thing of all!

My Great-aunt Alice, Miss Rumphius, is very old now. Her hair is very white. Every year there are more and more lupines. Now they call her the Lupine Lady. Sometimes my friends stand with me outside her gate, curious to see the old, old lady who planted the fields of lupines. When she invites us in, they come slowly. They think she is the oldest woman in the world. Often she tells us stories of faraway places.

"When I grow up," I tell her, "I too will go to faraway places and come home to live by the sea."

"That is all very well, little Alice," says my aunt, "but there is a third thing you must do."

"What is that?" I ask.

"You must do something to make the world more beautiful."

"All right," I say.
But I do not know yet what that can be.

Reader's Response ∼ What could you do to make the world more beautiful?

Library Link ∼ *To learn more about growing flowers, read* This Year's Garden *by Cynthia Rylant.*

Name That Plant!

Milkweed…silkweed…compass plant…morning glory. How did these flowers get their names?

◄ The leaves of the tall compass plant tend to point north and south. The compass plant is like a signpost on the prairie.

Break the stem of this plant and drops of milky fluid leak out. It's called milkweed. In the fall, brown milkweed seeds on silken parachutes float through the air. Another name for milkweed is silkweed! ►

◄ These flowers are in their glory in the morning. At sunset, they close their petals. People named them morning glories.

What name would you give to this flower? ►

Midori

by Helen Breen

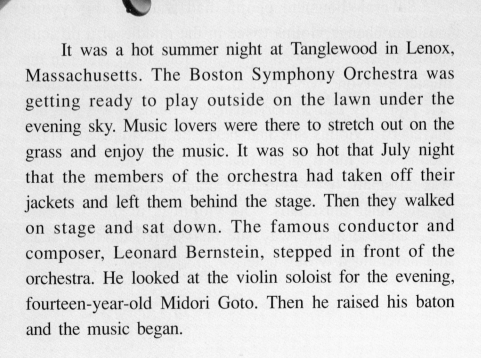

It was a hot summer night at Tanglewood in Lenox, Massachusetts. The Boston Symphony Orchestra was getting ready to play outside on the lawn under the evening sky. Music lovers were there to stretch out on the grass and enjoy the music. It was so hot that July night that the members of the orchestra had taken off their jackets and left them behind the stage. Then they walked on stage and sat down. The famous conductor and composer, Leonard Bernstein, stepped in front of the orchestra. He looked at the violin soloist for the evening, fourteen-year-old Midori Goto. Then he raised his baton and the music began.

The orchestra was playing *Serenade,* a musical selection that Mr. Bernstein had written. Both Mr. Bernstein and the members of the orchestra had pages of music in front of them. Only Midori played her part from memory. As Midori played, the sound of beautiful music filled the night air.

Then suddenly, one of the strings on Midori's violin broke. Quickly, Midori turned to the violinist seated behind her. He handed her his violin. She took it and continued playing. Within a minute, another string broke. Midori turned a second time to the violinist behind her. She hoped that he had put a new string on her violin, but he hadn't. All of his extra strings were offstage in his jacket pocket. Another violinist gave Midori his violin. Midori continued playing without making a mistake. When the music ended, the audience, Mr. Bernstein, and the members of the orchestra cheered Midori.

Several thousand people had watched this young musician change violins twice in the middle of a difficult musical piece. Never once did she forget her place in the music. Everyone was amazed.

Not only had Midori changed violins twice, she had played two violins she had never before touched. Those violins were much larger than her own. Because Midori was so small, her violin was smaller than those played by the other musicians. The violinists in the orchestra were amazed at the way she had switched violin sizes and never hit a wrong note.

The day after the Tanglewood concert, newspapers around the United States told the story. Midori's picture was on the front page of *The New York Times*. Reporters were eager to talk to her. They wanted to know how she felt when the strings on the violins broke. Was she scared? Midori replied, "What could I do? My strings broke, and I didn't want to stop the music."

Midori has loved music since she was a little girl. She began playing the violin when she was only four years old. Midori's mother, Sietsu Goto, was a violinist, too. She knew, even when Midori was very young, that Midori had a special talent. Midori and her mother lived in Japan at that time. When a famous American violin teacher, Dorothy DeLay, was visiting Japan, Mrs. Goto sent her a tape of Midori's violin playing.

Conductor Leonard Bernstein congratulates Midori.

Ms. DeLay listened to the tape and thought that Midori's playing was "extraordinary." Ms. DeLay wanted Midori and her mother to come to the United States so that Midori could study with her in New York. Even though it was hard to leave their home in Japan, Midori and her mother decided to move to New York. Midori was eleven at the time.

Midori attended the Professional Children's School in New York City. Most of her classmates there were actors and actresses. Midori found that school in the United States was different from school in Japan. She never knew any actors and actresses in Japan. Here, she often saw school friends on television.

Besides going to school, Midori practiced the violin four to five hours a day. She took extra classes at Juilliard, the most famous music school in the country. She also learned to play the piano and the viola. Midori studied the piano because it was required at Juilliard. But she learned the viola, which is like a large violin, just because she liked it.

Midori has always enjoyed many other things besides music. When she was eight, Midori saw a TV show about the Inca, people of South America who lived long ago. She began to read all she could about the Inca. She also wrote stories. Despite her fame, Midori liked to do many of the same things that you like to do. She liked to skip rope, jog, watch television, and read. She also liked to play with her cat and listen to popular music.

Today, Midori is famous throughout the world.

Some people would say that Midori's life is anything but ordinary. At the age of eleven she was the guest soloist with the Philadelphia Orchestra. When Midori came to rehearsal on the day of the concert, she looked out into the audience to make sure her teacher, Ms. DeLay, was there. Then she began to play the violin. Irvin Rosen, the leading violinist of the orchestra, described the way Midori played: "If I practiced three thousand years, I couldn't play like that. None of us could." That evening, when Midori finished her violin piece, the audience jumped to its feet and cheered. Four times Midori left the stage, but the audience kept calling her back.

Midori has been on television several times in programs about young musicians. She was also in a TV special, "Christmas at the White House," where she performed for the president. Midori has traveled throughout the United States and Europe to perform with well-known orchestras. Everywhere, music reviewers praise Midori's violin playing.

Midori has extraordinary talent. She plays difficult music very well. She is also a strong performer, able to go on with the show even when things go wrong. Her audiences know that they are listening to one of the best violinists of any age when Midori plays. Surely, Midori is one of a kind.

Reader's Response ∿ Midori has been famous since she was very young. Would you like to be famous? What would you like about it? What wouldn't you like?

The Gift of a Lifetime

Leonard Bernstein first dreamed of becoming a musician when his aunt gave the family an old piano. His piano teacher knew right away that Leonard had talent.

In college, Bernstein decided to become a composer. Then he later decided to become a conductor, too! His teachers were surprised. They had never heard of one person being a pianist, composer, and conductor at the same time.

When he was twenty-five, Bernstein became the assistant conductor of the New York Philharmonic Orchestra. One day a famous guest conductor got sick. It was up to Bernstein to lead the orchestra. When the concert was over, the audience cheered wildly. Suddenly, Bernstein was famous. He soon became America's most famous conductor.

During his life, he continued to play the piano and conduct the world's best orchestras. He also composed symphonies, jazz, ballet, and opera. Young people especially liked his television concerts for children.

The gift of a piano launched Bernstein's career. In turn, he gave everyone the gift of his wonderful music.

Ali Baba Bernstein

from *The Adventures of Ali Baba Bernstein*

by Johanna Hurwitz

David Bernstein was eight years, five months, and seventeen days old when he chose his new name.

There were already four Davids in David Bernstein's third-grade class. Every time his teacher, Mrs. Booxbaum, called, "David," all four boys answered. David didn't like that one bit. He wished he had an exciting name like one of the explorers he learned about in social studies—Vasco Da Gama. Once he found two unusual names on a program his parents brought home from a concert—Zubin Mehta and Wolfgang Amadeus Mozart. Now those were names with pizzazz!

David Bernstein might have gone along forever being just another David if it had not been for the book report that his teacher assigned.

"I will give extra credit for fat books," Mrs. Booxbaum told the class.

She didn't realize that all of her students would try to outdo one another. That afternoon when the third grade went to the school library, everyone tried to find the fattest book.

Melanie found a book with eighty pages.

Sam found a book with ninety-seven pages.

Jeffrey found a book with one hundred nineteen pages.

David K. and David S. each took a copy of the same book. It had one hundred forty-five pages.

None of the books were long enough for David Bernstein. He looked at a few that had over one hundred pages. He found one that had two hundred fourteen pages. But he wanted a book that had more pages than the total of all the pages in all the books his classmates were reading. He wanted to be the best student in the class—even in the entire school.

That afternoon he asked his mother what the fattest book was. Mrs. Bernstein thought for a minute. "I guess that would have to be the Manhattan telephone book," she said.

David Bernstein rushed to get the phone book. He lifted it up and opened to the last page. When he saw that it had over 1,578 pages, he was delighted.

He knew that no student in the history of P.S. 35 had ever read such a fat book. Just think how much extra credit he would get! David took the book and began to read name after name after name. After turning through all the *A* pages, he skipped to the name Bernstein. He found the listing for his father, Robert Bernstein. There were fifteen of them. Then he counted the number of David Bernsteins in the telephone book. There were seventeen. There was also a woman named Davida and a man named Davis, but he didn't count them. Right at that moment, David Bernstein decided two things: he would change his name and he would find another book to read.

The next day David went back to the school library. He asked the librarian to help him pick out a very fat book. "But it must be very exciting, too," he told her.

"I know just the thing for you," said the librarian.

She handed David a thick book with a bright red cover. It was *The Arabian Nights.* It had only three hundred thirty-seven pages, but it looked a lot more interesting than the phone book. David checked the book out of the library and spent the entire evening reading it. When he showed the book to his teacher the next day, she was very pleased.

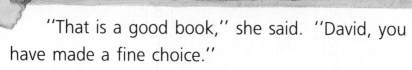

"That is a good book," she said. "David, you have made a fine choice."

It was at that moment that David Bernstein announced his new name. He had found it in the library book.

"From now on," David said, "I want to be called Ali Baba Bernstein."

Mrs. Booxbaum was surprised. David's parents were even more surprised. "David is a beautiful name," said his mother. "It was my grandfather's name."

"You can't just go around changing your name when you feel like it," his father said. "How will I ever know who I'm talking to?"

"You'll know it's still me," Ali Baba told his parents.

Mr. and Mrs. Bernstein finally agreed, although both of them frequently forgot and called their son David.

So now in Mrs. Booxbaum's class, there were three Davids and one Ali Baba. Ali Baba Bernstein was very happy. He was sure that a boy with an exciting name would have truly exciting adventures.

Only time would tell.

When Ali Baba Bernstein was eight years, eleven months, and four days old, his mother asked him how he wanted to celebrate his ninth birthday. He could take his friends to the bowling alley or to a movie. Or he could have a roller-skating party. None of these choices seemed very exciting to Ali Baba. Two boys in his class had already given bowling parties, another had invited all the boys in the class to a movie, and a third classmate was giving a roller-skating party next week. Ali Baba wanted to do something different.

"Do you remember when I counted all the David Bernsteins in the telephone book?"

Mrs. Bernstein nodded.

"I'd like to meet them all," said David. "I want to invite them here for my birthday."

"But you don't know them," his mother said. "And they are not your age."

"I want to see what they are all like," said Ali Baba. "If I can't invite them, then I don't want to have any party at all."

A week later, when Ali Baba was eight years, eleven months, and twelve days old, his mother asked about his birthday again.

"I told you what I decided," said Ali Baba.

That night Ali Baba's parents talked about the David Bernstein party. Mr. Bernstein liked his son's idea. He thought the other David Bernsteins might be curious to meet one another. So it was agreed that Ali Baba would have the party he wanted.

The very next morning, which was Saturday, Ali Baba and his father went to his father's office. Ali Baba had written an invitation to the David Bernstein party.

Dear David Bernstein:

I found your name in the Manhattan telephone book. My name is David Bernstein, too. I want to meet all the David Bernsteins in New York. I am having a party on Friday, May 12th at 7:00 P.M., and I hope you can come.

My mother is cooking supper. She is a good cook.

Yours truly,
David Bernstein
(also known as Ali Baba Bernstein)
P.S. May 12th is my ninth birthday, but you don't have to bring a present. RSVP: 211-3579

Mr. Bernstein had explained that RSVP was a French abbreviation that meant please tell me if you are going to come. He also said that his son should give his age in the letter.

"Honesty is the best policy, Ali Baba," his father advised.

Ali Baba was going to use the word processor in his father's office to print the letter. It took him a long time to type his letter on the machine. His father tried to help him, but he did not type very well either. When the letter was finally completed and the print button pushed, the machine produced seventeen perfect copies—one for each David Bernstein.

That evening Ali Baba addressed the seventeen envelopes so that the invitations could be mailed on Monday morning. His father supplied the stamps. By the end of the week, two David Bernsteins had already called to accept.

By the time Ali Baba Bernstein was eight years, eleven months, and twenty-nine days old, seven David Bernsteins had accepted his invitation. Four David Bernsteins called to say they couldn't come.

Six David Bernsteins did not answer at all.

Ali Baba and his mother chose the menu for his birthday dinner. There would be pot roast, corn (Ali Baba's favorite vegetable), rolls, applesauce, and salad. They were also having kasha varnishkas (a combination of buckwheat groats and noodles), which one of the guests had requested.

The evening of the party finally arrived. Ali Baba had decided to wear a pair of slacks, a sport jacket, and real dress shoes. It was not at all the way he would have dressed for a bowling party.

Ali Baba was surprised when the first guest arrived in a jogging suit and running shoes.

"How do you do," he said when Ali Baba opened the door. "I'm David Bernstein."

"Of course," said the birthday boy. "Call me Ali Baba."

Soon the living room was filled with David Bernsteins. They ranged in age from exactly nine years and three hours old to seventy-six years old (he was the David Bernstein who had asked for kasha varnishkas). There was a television director, a delicatessen owner, a mailman, an animal groomer, a dentist, a high-school teacher, and a writer. They all lived in Manhattan now, but they had been born in Brooklyn, the Bronx, Michigan, Poland, Germany, and South Africa. None of them had ever met any of the others before.

All of the guests enjoyed the dinner. "David, will you please pass those delicious rolls," asked the mailman.

"Certainly, David," said the animal groomer on his left.

"David, would you please pass the pitcher of apple cider this way," asked the dentist.

"Here it is, David," said the television director.

"I have trouble remembering names," the seventy-six-year-old David Bernstein told Ali Baba. "At this party I can't possibly forget." He smiled at Ali Baba. "What did you say your nickname was?"

"Ali Baba is not a nickname. I have chosen it to be my real name. There are too many David Bernsteins. There were even more in the telephone book who didn't come tonight."

"I was the only David Bernstein to finish the New York City Marathon," said David Bernstein the dentist. He was the one wearing running shoes.

"The poodles I clip don't care what my name is," said David Bernstein the animal groomer.

"It's not what you're called but what you do that matters," said the seventy-six-year-old David Bernstein.

All of them agreed to that.

"I once read that in some places children are given temporary names. They call them 'milk names.' They can then choose whatever names they want when they get older," said David Bernstein the high-school teacher.

"I'd still choose David Bernstein," said David Bernstein the delicatessen owner. "Just because we all have the same name doesn't make us the same."

"You're right," agreed David Bernstein the mailman.

"Here, here," called out David Bernstein the television director. He raised his glass of apple cider. "A toast to the youngest David Bernstein in the room."

Everyone turned to Ali Baba. He was about to say that he didn't want to be called David. But somehow he didn't mind his name so much now that he had met all these other David Bernsteins. They *were* all different. There would never be another David Bernstein like himself. One of these days he might go back to calling himself David again. But not just now.

"Open your presents," called out David Bernstein the writer.

Even though he had said that they didn't have to, several guests had brought gifts. So after singing "Happy Birthday" and cutting into the ice-cream cake that was shaped like the Manhattan phone book, Ali Baba began to open the packages. There was a pocket calculator the size of a business card, just like the one his father had. There was a jigsaw puzzle that looked like a subway map of Manhattan, a model airplane kit, and a few books. One was a collection of Sherlock Holmes stories. "I used to call myself Sherlock Bernstein," the high-school teacher recalled. There was an atlas and, best of all, there was *The Arabian Nights*.

"Now I have my own copy!" said Ali Baba. This was the best birthday he had ever had.

Finally, it was time for the guests to leave. "I never thought I would meet all the David Bernsteins," said David Bernstein the writer.

"You haven't," said Ali Baba. "Besides the seventeen David Bernsteins in the telephone book, there are six hundred eighty-three other Bernsteins listed between Aaron Bernstein and Zachary Bernstein. There must be members of their families who are named David. I bet there are thousands of David Bernsteins that I haven't met yet."

"You're right," said the seventy-six-year-old David Bernstein, patting Ali Baba on the back.

"Maybe I could invite them all next year," said Ali Baba. He was already nine years and six hours old.

"You could put an advertisement in the newspaper," suggested the mailman.

Ali Baba liked that idea.

David Bernstein the writer said, "I just might go home and write all about this. When did you get so interested in all the David Bernsteins?"

"It goes back a long time," said Ali Baba. "It all started on the day that I was eight years, five months, and seventeen days old."

Reader's Response ∼ If you had been David's friend, how would you have felt about his decision to change his name?

Library Link ∼ *This story is from* The Adventures of Ali Baba Bernstein *by Johanna Hurwitz. You might enjoy reading Ali Baba's other adventures in the book.*

What's in a Name?

*E*ric Thorvaldson, the Viking explorer, was called Eric the Red because of his red hair. His son Leif was known as Leif *Ericson*.

Many names have stories to tell. In some parts of Africa, for example, children are named for the day of the week they are born. In Ghana, if one of a boy's names is Kofi, you know he was born on a Friday.

In the United States, Pueblo children may be given two names, one when they are born and another a little later—a special Indian name. For example, Mary may also be called Ku-tsi-ya-t'si, which means Female Antelope.

In the Jewish tradition, some children may be given first names in memory of a relative.

Does your name have a story behind it?

Just Me

Nobody sees what I can see,
For back of my eyes there is only me.
And nobody knows how my thoughts begin,
For there's only myself inside my skin.

Isn't it strange how everyone owns
Just enough skin to cover his bones?
My father's would be too big to fit—
I'd be all wrinkled inside of it.
And my baby brother's is much too small—
It just wouldn't cover me up at all.
But I feel just right in the skin *I* wear,
And there's nobody like me anywhere.

Margaret Hillert

Lee Bennett Hopkins
INTERVIEWS
Beverly Cleary

Beverly Bunn Cleary was born in McMinnville, Oregon. Her father was a farmer, her mother a former schoolteacher. She spent the first six years of her life on a farm in Oregon. There, her mother would tell her every story, poem, folk tale, and fairy tale that she could remember.

"Reading meant so much to me as a child," Mrs. Cleary said. "I had read many books about wealthy English children who had nannies or rode in pony carts. *We* knew only about plowhorses! Other books I read were about poor children whose problems were solved by a long-lost, rich relative who turned up in the last chapter.

"I was fortunate to know a teacher-librarian who suggested that I write for children when I grew up. I wanted to read funny stories about the sort of children I knew, and I decided that someday I would write them."

After attending several colleges, Beverly Cleary became a children's librarian in Yakima, Washington. In 1940, she married Clarence Cleary, and they moved to Oakland, California. Upon moving into their new house, she found several piles of typing paper in a linen closet.

"Now I'll have to write a book," she told her husband.

"Why don't you?" he asked.

"Because we never have any sharp pencils," she answered. "The next day my husband went out and brought home a pencil sharpener. I realized that if I was ever going to write a book, this was the time to do it." The result has been the many books that she has created.

The Clearys now live in Carmel, California. They are the parents of grown twins, Marianne and Malcolm. I asked Mrs. Cleary what life was like in a house with a set of twins.

She replied, "Life with twins? It was busy! My novel *Mitch and Amy* came out of their experiences and the experiences of their friends when they were in the fourth grade."

Talking about her writing habits, she said, "Some parts of my stories come out right the first time; others I rewrite several times. A book should be the finished work of an author's imagination. If I start a book and do not like it, I just do not finish it. Writing is a pleasure, and I feel that if I didn't enjoy writing, no one would enjoy reading my books."

While working in Yakima with a group of boys who didn't care about reading, she heard the constant complaint that there weren't any books about "children like us." The boys wanted to read stories that showed the lives of ordinary children.

"Unless you count an essay I wrote about wild animals when I was ten years old, *Henry Huggins* was my first try at writing for children. When I wrote *Henry Huggins*, I wrote for all those little boys in Yakima," she said.

Since *Henry Huggins* appeared in 1950, Beverly Cleary has written close to thirty best-selling books for boys and girls, introducing such wonderful characters as Henry Huggins, Otis Spofford, Beezus, Ellen Tebbits, Ralph S. Mouse, Socks, Leigh Botts, Ramona Quimby and her family—all of whom have become true friends to readers for almost forty years.

Over the years Beverly Cleary has received many awards, including the 1984 Newbery Medal for *Dear Mr. Henshaw*.

The awards she cherishes most, however, are those that are voted on by children from various states. Two such awards she has received are the Mark Twain Award, chosen by children from Missouri, and the Nene Award, chosen by children from Hawaii.

''These awards are most meaningful to me,'' she says, ''because they come from my readers. I am deeply touched that so many girls and boys have voted for my books.''

One of the most delightful characters she has created is Ramona Quimby, who first appeared as a minor character in *Henry Huggins*. Over the years, Ramona became a girl readers loved and wanted to know more about. I asked Mrs. Cleary if there was a real Ramona whom she based her character on.

''Not really,'' she answered, ''although emotionally I was like Ramona growing up. I do have my Ramona side *and* my Ellen Tebbits side.''

The next story you will read is a selection from *Ramona and Her Father,* a 1978 Newbery Honor Book.

About reading, Beverly Cleary says, ''When you read, good things happen. Your life becomes more interesting and so do you. So grab a book. Read all kinds of books, and welcome the world.''

Reader's Response ∿ If you could ask Beverly Cleary one question, what would it be?

And the winner is...

How can you choose a good book at the library or bookstore? If a book has won an award, you know that many other people have enjoyed reading it or looking at its pictures.

In this country alone, there are about eighty awards given annually to writers and illustrators of children's books. Nearly twenty of these are chosen by young readers.

Here are some awards to look for:

◀ The Newbery Medal is given to the year's best writer of books for young people.

The Caldecott Medal is presented to the year's best illustrator of books for young people. ▶

◀ The Coretta Scott King Award goes to creative artists and authors whose work promotes world peace and brotherhood.

Ramona

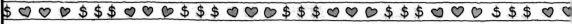

Ramona wished she had a million dollars so her father would be fun again. There had been many changes in the Quimby household since Mr. Quimby had lost his job, but the biggest change was in Mr. Quimby himself.

First of all, Mrs. Quimby found a full-time job working for another doctor, which was good news. However, even a second-grader could understand that one paycheck would not stretch as far as two paychecks, especially when there was so much talk of taxes, whatever they were. Mrs. Quimby's new job meant that Mr. Quimby had to be home when Ramona returned from school.

and the Million Dollars

from Ramona and Her Father
written by Beverly Cleary
illustrated by Alan Tiegreen

Ramona and her father saw a lot of one another. At first she thought having her father to herself for an hour or two every day would be fun, but when she came home, she found him running the vacuum cleaner, filling out job applications, or sitting on the couch, smoking and staring into space. He could not take her to the park because he had to stay near the telephone. Someone might call to offer him a job. Ramona grew uneasy. Maybe he was too worried to love her anymore.

One day Ramona came home to find her father in the living room drinking warmed-over coffee, smoking, and staring at the television set. On the screen a boy a couple of years younger than Ramona was singing:

Forget your pots,
   forget your pans.
It's not too late to
   change your plans.
Spend a little, eat a lot,
   Big fat burgers, nice and hot
   At your nearest Whopperburger!

Ramona watched him open his mouth wide to bite into a fat cheeseburger with lettuce and tomato spilling out of the bun and thought wistfully of the good old days when the family used to go to the restaurant on payday and when her mother used to bring home little treats—stuffed olives, cinnamon buns for Sunday breakfast, a bag of potato chips.

"That kid must be earning a million dollars." Mr. Quimby snuffed out his cigarette in a loaded ashtray. "He's singing that commercial every time I turn on television."

A boy Ramona's age earning a million dollars? Ramona was all interest. "How's he earning a million dollars?" she asked. She had often thought of all the things they could do if they had a million dollars, beginning with turning up the thermostat so they wouldn't have to wear sweaters in the house to save fuel oil.

Mr. Quimby explained. "They make a movie of him singing the commercial, and every time the movie is shown on television he gets paid. It all adds up."

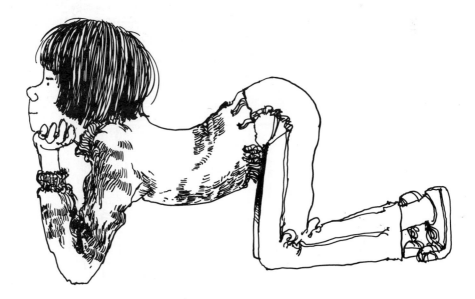

Well! This was a new idea to Ramona. She thought it over as she got out her crayons and paper and knelt on a chair at the kitchen table. Singing a song about hamburgers would not be hard to do. She could do it herself. Maybe she could earn a million dollars like that boy so her father would be fun again, and everyone at school would watch her on television and say, "There's Ramona Quimby. She goes to our school." A million dollars would buy a cuckoo clock for every room in the house, her father wouldn't need a job, the family could go to Disneyland....

"Forget your pots, forget your pans," Ramona began to sing, as she drew a picture of a hamburger and stabbed yellow dots across the top of the bun for sesame seeds. With a million dollars the Quimbys could eat in a restaurant every day if they wanted to.

After that Ramona began to watch for children on television commercials. She saw a boy eating bread and margarine when a crown suddenly appeared on his head with a fanfare—ta *da!*—of music. She saw a girl who asked, "Mommy, wouldn't it be nice if caramel apples grew on trees?" and another girl who took a bite of cereal said, "It's good, hm-um," and giggled. There was a boy who asked at the end of a weiner commercial, "Dad, how do you tell a boy hot dog from a girl hot dog?" and a girl who tipped her head to one side and said, "Pop-pop-pop," as she listened to her cereal. Children crunched potato chips, chomped on pickles, gnawed at fried chicken. Ramona grew particularly fond of the curly-haired little girl saying to her mother at the zoo, "Look, Mommy, the elephant's legs are wrinkled just like your pantyhose." Ramona could say all those things.

Ramona began to practice. Maybe someone would see her and offer her a million dollars to make a television commercial. On her way to school, if her friend Howie did not walk with her, she tipped her head to one side and said, "Pop-pop-pop." She said to herself, "M-m-m, it's good," and giggled. Giggling wasn't easy when she didn't have anything to giggle about, but she worked at it. Once she practiced on her mother by asking, "Mommy, wouldn't it be nice if caramel apples grew on trees?" She had taken to calling her mother Mommy lately, because children on commercials always called their mothers Mommy.

Mrs. Quimby's absentminded answer was, "Not really. Caramel is bad for your teeth." She was wearing slacks so Ramona could not say the line about pantyhose.

Since the Quimbys no longer bought potato chips or pickles, Ramona found other foods—toast and apples and carrot sticks—to practice good loud crunching on. When they had chicken for dinner, she smacked and licked her fingers.

"Ramona," said Mr. Quimby, "your table manners grow worse and worse. Don't eat so noisily. My grand-mother used to say, 'A smack at the table is worth a smack on the bottom.'"

Ramona, who did not think she would have liked her father's grandmother, was embarrassed. She had been practicing to be on television, and she had forgotten her family could hear.

Ramona continued to practice until she began to feel as if a television camera was watching her wherever she went. She smiled a lot and skipped, feeling that she was cute and lovable. She felt as if she had fluffy blond curls, even though in real life her hair was brown and straight.

One morning, smiling prettily, she thought, and swinging her lunch box, Ramona skipped to school. Today someone might notice her because she was wearing her red tights. She was happy because this was a special day, the day of Ramona's parent-teacher conference. Since Mrs. Quimby was at work, Mr. Quimby was going to meet with Mrs. Rogers, her second-grade teacher. Ramona was proud to have a father who would come to school.

Feeling dainty, curly-haired, and adorable, Ramona skipped into her classroom, and what did she see but Mrs. Rogers with wrinkles around her ankles. Ramona did not hesitate. She skipped right over to her teacher and, since there did not happen to be an elephant in Room 2, turned the words around and said, "Mrs. Rogers, your pantyhose are wrinkled like an elephant's legs."

Mrs. Rogers looked surprised, and the boys and girls who had already taken their seats giggled. All the teacher said was, "Thank you, Ramona, for telling me. And remember, we do not skip inside the school building."

Ramona had an uneasy feeling she had displeased her teacher.

She was sure of it when Howie said, "Ramona, you sure weren't very polite to Mrs. Rogers." Howie, a serious thinker, was usually right.

Suddenly Ramona was no longer an adorable little fluffy-haired girl on television. She was plain old Ramona, a second-grader whose own red tights bagged at the knee and wrinkled at the ankle. This wasn't the way things turned out on television. On television grown-ups always smiled at everything children said.

During recess Ramona went to the girls' bathroom and rolled her tights up at the waist to stretch them up at the knee and ankle. Mrs. Rogers must have done the same thing to her pantyhose, because after recess her ankles were smooth. Ramona felt better.

That afternoon, when the lower grades had been dismissed from their classrooms, Ramona found her father, along with Davy's mother, waiting outside the door of Room 2 for their conferences with Mrs. Rogers. Davy's mother's appointment was first, so Mr. Quimby sat down on a chair outside the door with a folder of Ramona's schoolwork to look over. Davy stood close to the door, hoping to hear what his teacher was saying about him. Everybody in Room 2 was anxious to learn what the teacher said.

Mr. Quimby opened Ramona's folder. "Run along and play on the playground until I'm through," he told his daughter.

"Promise you'll tell me what Mrs. Rogers says about me," said Ramona.

Mr. Quimby understood. He smiled and gave his promise.

Outside, the playground was chilly and damp. The only children who lingered were those whose parents had conferences, and they were more interested in what was going on inside the building than outside. Bored, Ramona looked around for something to do, and because she could find nothing better, she followed a traffic boy across the street. On the opposite side, near the market that had been built when she was in kindergarten, she decided she had time to explore. In a weedy space at the side of the market building, she discovered several burdock plants that bore a prickly crop of brown burs, each covered with sharp, little hooks.

Ramona saw at once that burs had all sorts of interesting possibilities. She picked two and stuck them together. She added another and another. They were better than Tinker-toys. She would have to tell Howie about them. When she had a string of burs, each clinging to the next, she bent it into a circle and stuck the ends together.

A crown! She could make a crown. She picked more burs and built up the circle by making peaks all the way around like the crown the boy wore in the margarine commercial. There was only one thing to do with a crown like that. Ramona crowned herself—ta-*da*!—like the boy on television.

Prickly though it was, Ramona enjoyed wearing the crown. She practiced looking surprised, like the boy who ate the margarine, and pretended she was rich and famous and about to meet her father, who would be driving a big shiny car bought with the million dollars she had earned.

The traffic boys had gone off duty. Ramona remembered to look both ways before she crossed the street, and as she crossed she pretended people were saying, "There goes that rich girl. She earned a million dollars eating margarine on TV."

Mr. Quimby was standing on the playground, looking for Ramona. Forgetting all she had been pretending, Ramona ran to him. "What did Mrs. Rogers say about me?" she demanded.

"That's some crown you've got there," Mr. Quimby remarked.

"Daddy, what did she *say?*"

Ramona could not contain her impatience.

Mr. Quimby grinned. "She said you were impatient."

Oh, that. People were always telling Ramona not to be so impatient. "What else?" asked Ramona, as she and her father walked toward home.

"You are a good reader, but you are careless about spelling."

Ramona knew this. Unlike Beezus, who was an excellent speller, Ramona could not believe spelling was important as long as people could understand what she meant. "What else?"

"She said you draw unusually well for a second-grader and your printing is the best in the class."

"What else?"

Mr. Quimby raised one eyebrow as he looked down at Ramona. "She said you were inclined to show off and you sometimes forget your manners."

Ramona was indignant at this criticism. "I do not! She's just making that up." Then she remembered what she had said about her teacher's pantyhose and felt subdued. She hoped her teacher had not repeated her remark to her father.

"I remember my manners most of the time," said Ramona, wondering what her teacher had meant by showing off. Being first to raise her hand when she knew the answer?

"Of course you do," agreed Mr. Quimby. "After all, you are my daughter. Now tell me, how are you going to get that crown off?"

Using both hands, Ramona tried to lift her crown but only succeeded in pulling her hair. The tiny hooks clung fast. Ramona tugged. Ow! That hurt. She looked helplessly up at her father.

Mr. Quimby appeared amused. "Who do you think you are? A Rose Festival Queen?"

Ramona pretended to ignore her father's question. How silly to act like someone on television when she was a plain old second-grader whose tights bagged at the knees again. She hoped her father would not guess. He might. He was good at guessing.

By then Ramona and her father were home. As Mr. Quimby unlocked the front door, he said, "We'll have to see what we can do about getting you uncrowned before your mother gets home. Any ideas?"

Ramona had no answer, although she was eager to part with the crown before her father guessed what she had been doing. In the kitchen, Mr. Quimby picked off the top of the crown, the part that did not touch Ramona's hair. That was easy. Now came the hard part.

"Yow!" said Ramona, when her father tried to lift the crown.

"That won't work," said her father. "Let's try one bur at a time." He went to work on one bur, carefully trying to untangle it from Ramona's hair, one strand at a time.

To Ramona, who did not like to stand still, this process took forever. Each bur was snarled in a hundred hairs, and each hair had to be pulled before the bur was loosened. After a very long time, Mr. Quimby handed a hair-entangled bur to Ramona.

"Yow! Yipe! Leave me some hair," said Ramona, picturing a bald circle around her head.

"I'm trying," said Mr. Quimby and began on the next bur.

Ramona sighed. Standing still doing nothing was tiresome.

After what seemed like a long time, Beezus came home from school. She took one look at Ramona and began to laugh.

"I don't suppose you ever did anything dumb," said Ramona, short of patience and anxious lest her sister guess why she was wearing the remains of a crown. "What about the time you—"

"No arguments," said Mr. Quimby. "We have a problem to solve, and it might be a good idea if we solved it before your mother comes home from work."

Much to Ramona's annoyance, her sister sat down to watch. "How about soaking?" suggested Beezus. "It might soften all those millions of little hooks."

"Yow! Yipe!" said Ramona. "You're pulling too hard."

Mr. Quimby laid another hair-filled bur on the table. "Maybe we should try. This isn't working."

"It's about time she washed her hair anyway," said Beezus, a remark Ramona felt was entirely unnecessary. Nobody could shampoo hair full of burs.

Ramona knelt on a chair with her head in a sinkful of warm water for what seemed like hours until her knees ached and she had a crick in her neck. "Now, Daddy?" she asked at least once a minute.

"Not yet," Mr. Quimby answered, feeling a bur. "Nope," he said at last. "This isn't going to work."

Ramona lifted her dripping head from the sink. When her father tried to dry her hair, the bur hooks clung to the towel. He jerked the towel loose and draped it around Ramona's shoulders.

"Well, live and learn," said Mr. Quimby. "Beezus, scrub some potatoes and throw them in the oven. We can't have your mother come home and find we haven't started supper."

When Mrs. Quimby arrived, she took one look at her husband trying to untangle Ramona's wet hair from the burs, groaned, sank limply onto a kitchen chair, and began to laugh.

By now Ramona was tired, cross, and hungry. "I don't see anything funny," she said sullenly.

Mrs. Quimby managed to stop laughing. "What on earth got into you?" she asked.

Ramona considered. Was this a question grown-ups asked just to be asking a question, or did her mother expect an answer? "Nothing," was a safe reply. She would never tell her family how she happened to be wearing a crown of burs. Never, not even if they threw her into a dungeon.

"Beezus, bring me the scissors," said Mrs. Quimby.

Ramona clapped her hands over the burs. "No!" she shrieked and stamped her foot. "I won't let you cut off my hair! I won't! I won't! I won't!"

Beezus handed her mother the scissors and gave her sister some advice. "Stop yelling. If you go to bed with burs in your hair, you'll really get messed up."

Ramona had to face the wisdom of Beezus's words. She stopped yelling to consider the problem once more. "All right," she said, as if she were granting a favor, "but I want Daddy to do it." Her father would work with care while her mother, always in a hurry since she was working full time, would go *snip-snip-snip* and be done with it. Besides, supper would be prepared faster and would taste better if her mother did the cooking.

"I am honored," said Mr. Quimby. "Deeply honored."

Mrs. Quimby did not seem sorry to hand over the scissors.

"Why don't you go someplace else to work while Beezus and I get supper on the table?"

Mr. Quimby led Ramona into the living room, where he turned on the television set. "This may take time," he explained, as he went to work. "We might as well watch the news."

Ramona was still anxious. "Don't cut any more than you have to, Daddy," she begged, praying the margarine boy would not appear on the screen. "I don't want everyone at school to make fun of me." The newscaster was talking about strikes and a lot of things Ramona did not understand.

"The merest smidgin," promised her father. *Snip. Snip. Snip.* He laid a hair-ensnarled bur in an ashtray. *Snip. Snip. Snip.* He laid another bur beside the first.

"Does it look awful?" asked Ramona.

"As my grandmother would say, 'It will never be noticed from a trotting horse.' "

Ramona let out a long, shuddery sigh, the closest thing to crying without really crying. *Snip. Snip. Snip.* Ramona touched the side of her head. She still had hair there. More hair than she expected. She felt a little better.

The newscaster disappeared from the television screen, and there was that boy again singing:

Forget your pots,
    forget your pans.
It's not too late to
    change your plans.

Ramona thought longingly of the days before her father lost his job, when they could forget their pots and pans and change their plans. She watched the boy open his mouth wide and sink his teeth into that fat hamburger with lettuce, tomato, and cheese hanging out of the bun. She swallowed and said, "I bet that boy has a lot of fun with his million dollars." She felt so sad. The Quimbys really needed a million dollars. Even one dollar would help.

Snip. Snip. Snip. "Oh, I don't know," said Mr. Quimby. "Money is handy, but it isn't everything."

"I wish I could earn a million dollars like that boy," said Ramona. This was the closest she would ever come to telling how she happened to set a crown of burs on her head.

"You know something?" said Mr. Quimby. "I don't care how much that kid or any other kid earns. I wouldn't trade you for a million dollars."

"Really, Daddy?" That remark about any other kid—Ramona wondered if her father had guessed her reason for the crown, but she would never ask. Never. "Really? Do you mean it?"

"Really." Mr. Quimby continued his careful snipping. "I'll bet that boy's father wishes he had a little girl who finger-painted and wiped her hands on the cat when she was little and who once cut her own hair so she would be bald like her uncle and who then grew up to be seven years old and crowned herself with burs. Not every father is lucky enough to have a daughter like that."

Ramona giggled. "Daddy, you're being silly!" She was happier than she had been in a long time.

Reader's Response ～ Would you like to have Ramona Quimby as a friend? What would you like about her? What things might you not like about her?

Library Link ～ *This story is taken from the book* Ramona and Her Father *by Beverly Cleary. You might enjoy reading the rest of the book to find out what happens to Ramona and her million dollar dream.*

Gather 'Round

*S*tories are fun to read,
  fun to hear, and fun to tell.

What is a good story
  that you know?

JUNGLE TALES (CONTES DE LA JUNGLE), *oil on canvas by James Jebusa Shannon, American, 1895, 34 1/4" x 44 3/4", Arthur Hoppock Hearn Fund, 1913, 13.143.1, © The Metropolitan Museum of Art, New York*

Theme Books for
Gather 'Round

*D*o you remember a story so good that you couldn't wait for the storyteller to say the next word or turn the page?

◆ ***The Boy and the Ghost*** by Robert D. San Souci is a tale of courage that will make your spine tingle. If Thomas can stay overnight in a haunted house, he might win the secret treasure!

You will find even stranger happenings in a tall tale by Susan Pearson, **Well, I Never!** Welcome to a wild farm, where floating pigs blow bubbles and cows wear clothes! How will this farm family deal with such amazing events?

More Books to Enjoy

The Six Swans by Robert D. San Souci
Why Spiders Spin by Jamie and Scott Simons
The Gift of the Sacred Dog by Paul Goble
Cherries and Cherry Pits by Vera B. Williams

A STORY A STORY

retold and illustrated by Gail E. Haley

Many African stories, whether or not they are about Kwaku Ananse the "spider man," are called "Spider Stories." This book is about how that came to be.

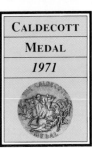

"Spider Stories" tell how small, defenseless men or animals outwit others and succeed against great odds. These stories crossed the Atlantic Ocean in the cruel ships that delivered slaves to the Americas. Their descendants still tell some of these stories today. Ananse has become Anancy in the Caribbean isles, while he survives as "Aunt Nancy" in the southern United States.

You will find many African words in this story. If you listen carefully, you can tell what they mean by their sounds. At times words and phrases are repeated several times. Africans repeat words to make them stronger. For example: "So small, so small, so small," means very, very, very small.

The African storyteller begins:

"We do not really mean, we do not really mean that what we are about to say is true. A story, a story; let it come, let it go."

Once, oh small children round my knee, there were no stories on earth to hear. All the stories belonged to Nyame, the Sky God. He kept them in a golden box next to his royal stool.

Ananse, the spider man, wanted to buy the Sky God's stories. So he spun a web up to the sky.

When the Sky God heard what Ananse wanted, he laughed: "Twe, twe, twe. The price of my stories is that you bring me Osebo the leopard of-the-terrible-teeth, Mmboro the hornet who-stings-like-fire, and Mmoatia the fairy whom-men-never-see."

Ananse bowed and answered: "I shall gladly pay the price."

"Twe, twe, twe," chuckled the Sky God. "How can a weak old man like you, so small, so small, so small, pay my price?"

But Ananse merely climbed down to earth to find the things that the Sky God demanded.

Ananse ran along the jungle path—yiridi, yiridi, yiridi—till he came to Osebo the leopard-of-the-terrible-teeth.

"Oho, Ananse," said the leopard, "you are just in time to be my lunch."

Ananse replied: "As for that, what will happen will happen. But first let us play the binding binding game."

The leopard, who was fond of games, asked: "How is it played?"

"With vine creepers," explained Ananse. "I will bind you by your foot and foot. Then I will untie you, and you can tie me up."

"Very well," growled the leopard, who planned to eat Ananse as soon as it was his turn to bind him.

So Ananse tied the leopard by his foot by his foot by his foot by his foot, with the vine creeper. Then he said: "Now, Osebo, you are ready to meet the Sky God." And he hung the tied leopard in a tree in the jungle.

Next Ananse cut a frond from a banana tree and filled a calabash with water. He crept through the tall grasses, sora, sora, sora, till he came to the nest of Mmboro, the hornets-who-sting-like-fire.

Ananse held the banana leaf over his head as an umbrella. Then he poured some of the water in the calabash over his head.

The rest he emptied over the hornet's nest and cried: "It is raining, raining, raining. Should you not fly into my calabash, so that the rain will not tatter your wings?"

"Thank you. Thank you," hummed the hornets, and they flew into the calabash—fom! Ananse quickly stopped the mouth of the gourd.

"Now, Mmboro, you are ready to meet the Sky God," said Ananse. And he hung the calabash full of hornets onto the tree next to the leopard.

Ananse now carved a little wooden doll holding a bowl. He covered the doll from top to bottom with sticky latex gum. Then he filled the doll's bowl with pounded yams.

He set the little doll at the foot of a flamboyant tree where fairies like to dance. Ananse tied one end of a vine round the doll's head and, holding the other end in his hand, he hid behind a bush.

In a little while, Mmoatia the fairy-whom-no-man-sees came dancing, dancing, dancing, to the foot of the flamboyant tree. There she saw the doll holding the bowl of yams.

Mmoatia said: "Gum baby, I am hungry. May I eat some of your yams?"

Ananse pulled at the vine in his hiding place, so that the doll seemed to nod its head. So the fairy took the bowl from the doll and ate all the yams.

"Thank you, Gum baby," said the fairy. But the doll did not answer.

"Don't you reply when I thank you?" cried the angered fairy. The doll did not stir.

"Gum baby, I'll slap your crying place unless you answer me," shouted the fairy. But the wooden doll remained still and silent. So the fairy slapped her crying place—pa! Her hand stuck fast to the gum baby's sticky cheek.

"Let go of my hand, or I'll slap you again." —Pa! She slapped the doll's crying place with her other hand. Now the fairy was stuck to the gum baby with both hands, and she was furious. She pushed against the doll with her feet, and they also stuck fast.

Now Ananse came out of hiding. "You are ready to meet the Sky God, Mmoatia." And he carried her to the tree where the leopard and the hornets were waiting.

Ananse spun a web round Osebo, Mmboro,
and Mmoatia. Then he spun a web to the sky. He
pulled up his captives behind him, and set them
down at the feet of the Sky God.

"O, Nyame," said Ananse, bowing low, "here
is the price you ask for your stories: Osebo the
leopard-of-the-terrible-teeth, Mmboro the hornets-
who-sting-like-fire, and Mmoatia the fairy-whom-
men-never-see."

Nyame the Sky God called together all the nobles of his court and addressed them in a loud voice: "Little Ananse, the spider man, has paid me the price I ask for my stories. Sing his praise. I command you."

"From this day and going on forever," proclaimed the Sky God, "my stories belong to Ananse and shall be called 'Spider Stories.'"

"Eeeee, Eeeee, Eeeee," shouted all the assembled nobles.

So Ananse took the golden box of stories back to earth, to the people of his village. And when he opened the box all the stories scattered to the corners of the world, including this one.

This is my story which I have related. If it be sweet, or if it be not sweet, take some elsewhere, and let some come back to me.

Reader's Response ∾ Would you have treated the animals the same way Ananse did? Why or why not?

Library Link ∾ *You can read other stories about Ananse in* Oh, Kojo! How Could You! *by Verna Aardema.*

ALONG CAME A SPIDER

A Greek myth tells about a young woman named Arachne, who spun the most beautiful cloth that anyone had ever seen. She boasted that she was more skillful than the goddess Athena. After the two had a weaving contest that came out even, Athena changed Arachne into a spider destined to spin webs forevermore. Today *Arachnida* is the scientific name for the animal group of which spiders are a member.

According to a Japanese legend, fleecy clouds are spun in the sky by Spider-girl. In fact, even today a spider and a cloud have the same name in Japanese: *kumo*.

American Indians associated spiders with the sun because the rays of their webs stretch out like sunbeams. The Apaches honored Grandfather Spider, saying that he wove a ladder of sunbeams so that people could climb up from the center of the earth and live in daylight.

Spiders were spinning webs before mammals and birds appeared on earth. Is it any wonder that spider stories are found around the world?

The Traveling Storyteller

by Linda Goss

Storytelling is an art form that brings people together. All over the world, people love to listen to stories. I love to tell stories. My name is Linda Goss. I am a traveling storyteller.

I was born near the Great Smoky Mountains in Alcoa, Tennessee. All the members of my family loved stories, so I grew up with storytelling. My mother told me stories from the Bible. My favorite one was about a man named Jonah, who was swallowed by a whale. My father told me funny versions of popular fairy tales, such as Cinderella.

Perhaps my grandfather's stories had the greatest influence on me. I called my grandfather "Grand-daddy Murphy." He told me all kinds of stories, especially tales of his childhood and folk tales he remembered hearing when he was a boy. Grand-daddy Murphy's favorite folk tales were about "Brer Rabbit." Brer Rabbit was a clever animal who often played tricks on Brer Bear and Brer Fox. "But sometimes Brer Rabbit's cleverness got the best of him," Grand-daddy Murphy would say as he ended a story. I would laugh and he would tell me another one.

I have forgotten some of the stories my family told me. The ones I do remember I have passed down to my daughters, Aisha and Uhuru, and my son, Jamaal. I hope they will pass down the stories to their children, and so on, and so on.

◀ **Linda Goss gets ready to tell a story.**

How I Became a Professional Storyteller

I have always kept the love for storytelling deep inside me. So, I decided to become a professional storyteller and share my stories with the world. A professional storyteller is a person who earns a living by telling stories. I became a professional storyteller in Washington, D.C., in 1973. At that time, my husband, Clay Goss, was teaching at Howard University. One day he came home from work and said, "Linda, the university is looking for a storyteller." I answered, "Well, here I am!"

I was used to telling stories to my children at home, but not to strangers. Would I be able to do it? Then the moment came when I was on stage. I looked at the audience. They were all looking at me. I was very nervous. I was scared, too. But as I thought about the stories, I forgot how scared and nervous I was. When I finished, the audience clapped. They said that they liked the way I told stories. Suddenly, they no longer seemed like strangers to me. From that day on I knew I would always tell stories.

While I was in Washington, D.C., I was invited to tell stories at the Martin Luther King, Jr., Library, the Smithsonian Institution, and even at President's Park on the White House lawn. Then my family and I moved from Washington, D.C., to Philadelphia, Pennsylvania. No one there knew I was a professional storyteller, so I decided to return to teaching.

I told stories to my students every day. Before long, their parents wanted me to tell them stories at workshops and churches. Other teachers in the school wanted me to tell them stories in workshops, too. Soon, other schools were inviting me to come and tell stories.

◄ **Linda Goss is telling an Ananse story to a group of students at a school in Philadelphia, Pennsylvania.**

Some people who liked my stories formed a group called "Friends of Linda Goss." They invited me to tell stories at a library in Germantown, a neighborhood in Philadelphia. Five hundred people came to hear me. The next thing I knew, I was telling stories everywhere. I traveled on airplanes, trains, and riverboats to get to places where I had been invited to tell stories. I had become a traveling storyteller.

Where I Find Stories

I find stories in many different places and get them in many different ways. I get them from books, friends, other storytellers, and from countries around the world. Some of the stories I tell are folk tales. These are stories that have been passed down from one generation to the next. Folk tales were first told aloud. They were not written down for many, many years. Some of the folk tales I enjoy telling are "how and why" tales. A "how and why" tale tries to explain how or why something came to be. For example, it may tell how the elephant got its long trunk, or why bears have short tails. I also make up some of my stories, and sometimes, my husband writes stories for me.

My favorite stories come from Ghana, a country in West Africa. That is where Ananse the Spider is supposed to have come from. I have been telling Ananse stories for over ten years. Some people say that Ananse was the first storyteller. There are thousands of stories about him, like the one you read in this book.

How I Tell Stories

I try to make my storytelling programs exciting and special. I always begin by ringing large bells. Then I chant, "Story, storytelling time." This lets the audience know that it is time to listen. I wear brightly colored gowns. Most of these gowns are made out of cloths from Africa. They have drawings on them of birds, fish, butterflies, and yes, even Ananse the Spider.

Linda Goss uses cloth from Africa to make her storytelling gowns. ▶

When I tell Ananse stories, I try to move my arms and fingers as Ananse might have. I try to show different expressions on my face, as Ananse might have.

I carry a "goodie bag" full of cloths when I tell stories. These cloths come from many different countries. I use the cloths to help tell stories. One cloth might become the wind, another a rain forest. I even carry an Ananse cloth in my goodie bag.

The audience also helps me tell stories. They help me create a special place by moving their arms and making sounds that animals make. They move around and sing, and pretend to become the animal characters in the stories. The audience and I have a wonderful time together. To me, that is what storytelling is all about.

Reader's Response ～ Would you like to hear Linda Goss tell one of her stories? How might listening to her tell the story be different from reading it yourself?

Library Link ～ *You may not be able to hear Linda Goss tell her stories, but you can read ones like them yourself. Try* Tales of an Ashanti Father, *retold by Peggy Appiah.*

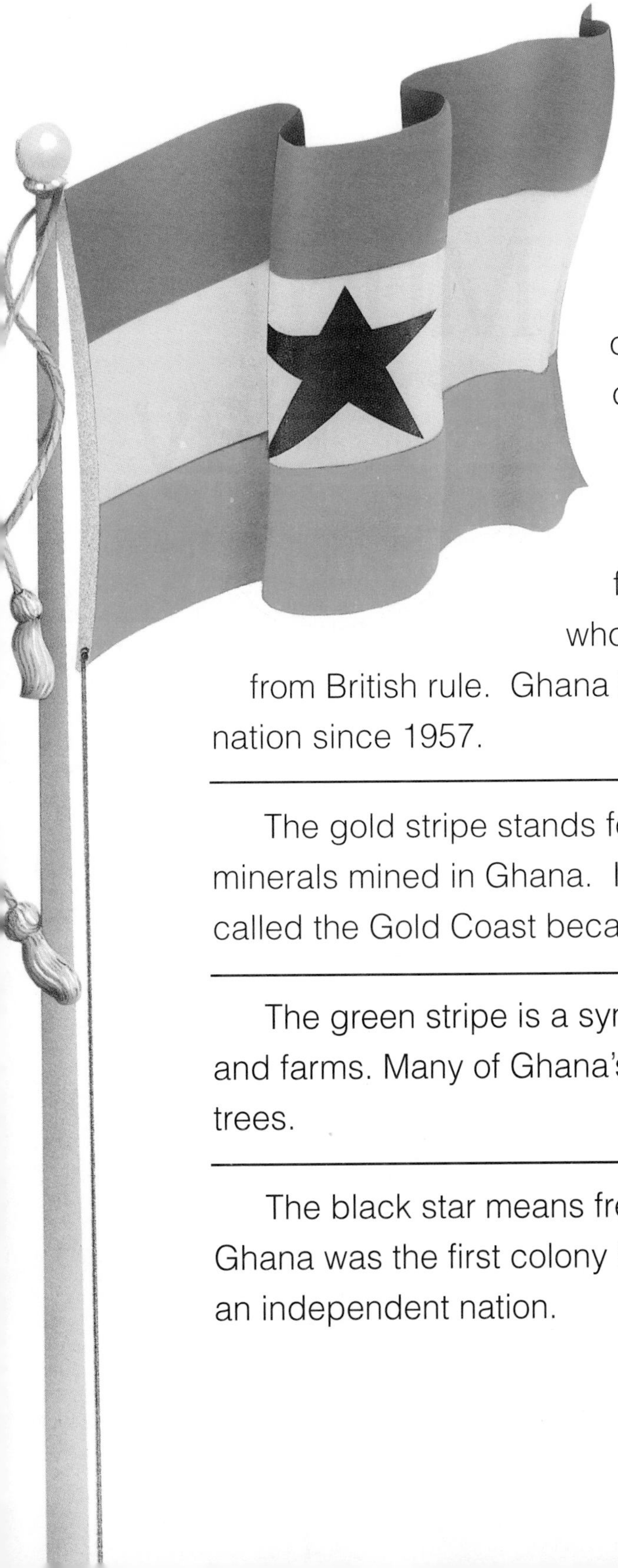

Flying Colors

Ghana's flag is as colorful as its traditional cloth. The flag also tells a story.

The red stripe in the flag honors the people who fought for independence from British rule. Ghana has been an independent nation since 1957.

The gold stripe stands for the gold and other minerals mined in Ghana. In fact, Ghana used to be called the Gold Coast because of its gold resources.

The green stripe is a symbol of Ghana's forests and farms. Many of Ghana's farmers raise cacao trees.

The black star means freedom and shows that Ghana was the first colony in Black Africa to become an independent nation.

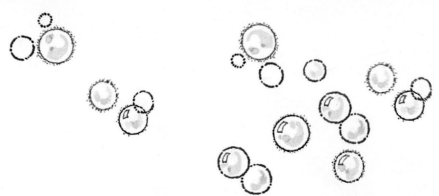

Nothing Much Happened Today

by Mary Blount Christian

Mrs. Maeberry held her groceries tightly.
She scurried home to tell her children about
seeing the police chase a robber. But when she
turned down her sidewalk, her mouth flew open.
Soap bubbles—hundreds, thousands, maybe
millions of soap bubbles—were drifting from her
front window. She ran inside. "What's
happened?" she demanded. "What's happened
here?"

Stephen shrugged. "Nothing much, really."

"But the bubbles!" she yelled. "Look at
those bubbles!"

Stephen shrugged again.

Elizabeth mumbled, "I guess maybe we did use too many suds when we bathed Popsicle."

"The dog? You bathed the dog?" Mother screamed. "Why did you bathe the dog?"

"He got sugar stuck all over his fur," Alan, the youngest, said.

Mother set her groceries down. "I was gone five minutes, just five minutes. How could Popsicle get sugar in his fur?"

"He got sugar in his fur when he knocked over the sugar sack. That was when he was chasing the cat through the kitchen," Stephen added.

Mother gasped. "Cat? Cat? We don't *have* a cat."

"I guess you could say it was a visiting cat,"
Stephen explained. "It came through the
window."

"The window?" Mother shrieked. "That cat
broke the glass?"

Stephen shook his head. "Nope. The
window was open. We had to let the smoke
out."

Mother grabbed her forehead. "Smoke!
What smoke?"

"The smoke from the oven when the cake
batter spilled over," Elizabeth volunteered.

Mother waved her arms. "Why were you
baking a cake?"

"For the school bake sale," Alan reminded
her.

"But," Mother protested. "But I baked that before I went to the store."

"We know," Stephen said, "but that one got ruined."

"Ruined?" Mother repeated. "How could my beautiful cake get ruined? I was gone ten minutes, only ten minutes."

"The cake was knocked onto the floor, and it's a good thing it was, too," Elizabeth said.

"I don't understand this. I don't understand this at all," Mother said.

"It's not so bad," Stephen said. "We used too many soap suds on Popsicle because he was covered with sugar. He knocked the sugar over chasing the cat. The cat came through the window when we let out the smoke. The smoke is from the spilled cake batter in the oven. We were replacing the cake you baked because that one got knocked off by the policeman."

Mother's eyebrows shot up. "Policeman! What policeman?"

"The policeman that ran in after the robber," Alan told her.

"MY robber?" Mother gasped. "I—I mean the grocery robber?" She sank into a chair. "But tell me, please. Tell me how a robber and a policeman ruined my cake."

Stephen smiled. "That's easy. The robber ran around and around our kitchen table. The policeman went around and around after him. The policeman accidentally knocked the cake to the floor. The robber skidded in the icing."

Elizabeth interrupted. "And when the robber fell, he hit his head on Alan's head. And you know how hard Alan's head is."

"I know. I know," Mother said. "Let me see now. The robber ran into here and the policeman chased him. They ruined the cake. When you baked a new one you made the oven smokey. Then you opened the window to let the smoke out and the cat came in. Popsicle chased the cat and knocked the sack of sugar on himself. And that's when you bathed him with too many suds?"

"That's right," the three children said together. "And that's when you came home."

"Twenty minutes at the most," Mother said. "I *know* I couldn't have been gone more than 20 minutes, anyway."

"We *told* you nothing much happened today," Stephen said. "How was your day?"

"Nothing much," Mother said, sliding further back into the chair. "Nothing much." The last soap bubble floated gently to the end of her nose where it rested, then popped, and was gone.

Reader's Response ~ Which part of this story do you think would make the funniest cartoon?

Silly Stuff

What makes you laugh?

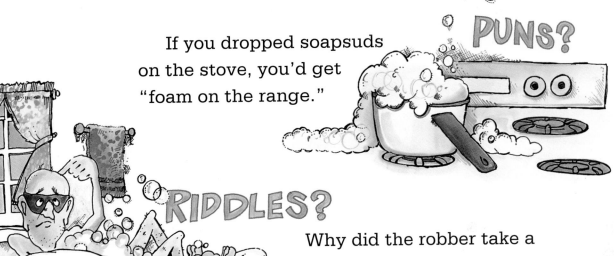

If you dropped soapsuds on the stove, you'd get "foam on the range."

PUNS?

RIDDLES?

Why did the robber take a bath? (He wanted to make a clean getaway.)

KNOCK KNOCK JOKES?

Knock, knock.
Who's there?
Howie.
Howie who?
Howie going to explain this mess to Mother?

Also check out limericks and elephant jokes. Then share some silly stuff with a friend.

King Midas
and the Golden Touch

Retold by
Judy Rosenbaum

Once upon a time there was a very rich king named Midas. He lived in a fine castle with his daughter, Marygold. The two things he loved best in life were gold and Marygold. He loved to go into his treasure room and count his coins. No one, not even Marygold, was allowed into the king's treasure room.

One day Midas was sitting in the treasure room dreaming about his gold. In his dream, he saw a shadow fall across the piles of valuable gold coins. He looked up and saw a stranger standing near him. Since no one was allowed into his treasure room, Midas was surprised. The stranger looked kind, however, so Midas wasn't afraid. He greeted the man, and they began to talk of gold.

"You certainly have a lot of gold," said the stranger.

"It's not so much," said Midas.

The stranger smiled. "Do you want even more gold than this?" he asked.

"If I had my way, everything I touched would turn into gold," Midas replied.

The stranger's smile grew wider. "So you want the Golden Touch? Very well, I will give it to you. At sunrise tomorrow, you will be able to turn anything you touch into gold."

Midas was so excited that he could hardly wait until morning. At last the sun rose. Still dreaming, Midas sat up and reached for the water jug by his bed. At once it became gold. Midas was so overjoyed, he got up and danced around the room, touching everything within his reach. Soon, he had a room full of gleaming gold objects. When he reached for his clothes, they turned into heavy golden cloth. "Now I shall really look like a king," he said. He got dressed and admired himself in the mirror. Midas was impressed by his golden clothes, though they were so heavy he could hardly move.

His looking glass was more of a problem. He tried to use it to see his new treasures better. To his surprise, he could not see anything through it. He put it on the table and found that it was now gold, but Midas was too excited to worry. He said, "I can see well enough without it. Besides, it is much more valuable now."

Midas went down to his rose garden. There, he touched rosebush after rosebush. Soon, one whole corner of the garden was filled with golden roses. Their bright petals reflected the sun, and their stems had become thin gold wires. Even the thorns on the rosebushes had turned into gold. Midas was completely happy.

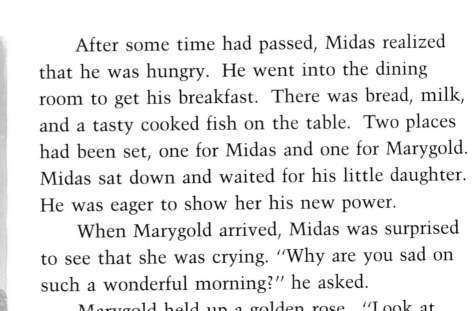

After some time had passed, Midas realized that he was hungry. He went into the dining room to get his breakfast. There was bread, milk, and a tasty cooked fish on the table. Two places had been set, one for Midas and one for Marygold. Midas sat down and waited for his little daughter. He was eager to show her his new power.

When Marygold arrived, Midas was surprised to see that she was crying. "Why are you sad on such a wonderful morning?" he asked.

Marygold held up a golden rose. "Look at what has happened to the flowers in our lovely garden," she said. "Our roses have no smell anymore. Their petals have become hard, with sharp edges, and they have such an ugly color!"

Midas was too ashamed to tell Marygold how the roses had become hard and golden. So he just said, "Now, now, Marygold, everything will be all right."

Marygold sat down, but she didn't cheer up. She was so upset that she didn't notice what was going on at the table. Midas was having a lot of trouble with his breakfast. When he took a piece of bread, it turned into a golden lump in his hand. The fish became a beautiful, but useless, golden fish with tiny gold bones. The milk in his cup hardened into metal when his lips touched it. "If this goes on, I'll never be able to eat again," said poor Midas.

Marygold looked up. "Father, what's wrong?" she asked. Then she saw all the shining food on the gleaming dishes in front of her father. "Oh, poor Father," she said. She gave him some of her food, but it too turned into gold. Marygold felt terrible for her father. She hurried over to comfort him. As she threw her arms around him, Midas let out a warning cry, but it was too late. His daughter had turned into a silent golden statue. Even the tears on her cheeks had turned into tiny drops of gold. "Oh, what a terrible thing I have done!" cried Midas.

Midas, with great sadness, sat next to poor Marygold for a long time. After a while, he heard someone in the doorway. He looked up. There stood the stranger in his dream. "I see the Golden Touch has not made you happy," the stranger said gently.

"I would do anything to get rid of this terrible gift," Midas said.

The stranger said, "Go and wash yourself in the river. Then splash water from the river on everything that you turned into gold."

Midas thanked the stranger, grabbed a huge jug, and rushed outside. When he ran through the garden, more roses turned to gold as he brushed past them. Midas reached the river and walked in. He stayed there for a long time before getting out. Then he nervously touched a flower growing along the river. It did not change to gold. "I'm cured!" Midas shouted. He picked up his gold jug and filled it with water. At once it became an ordinary jug again. Midas ran with the jug to Marygold. As soon as he poured the water on his beloved daughter, her skin became soft, and she began to move. Midas hugged her joyfully.

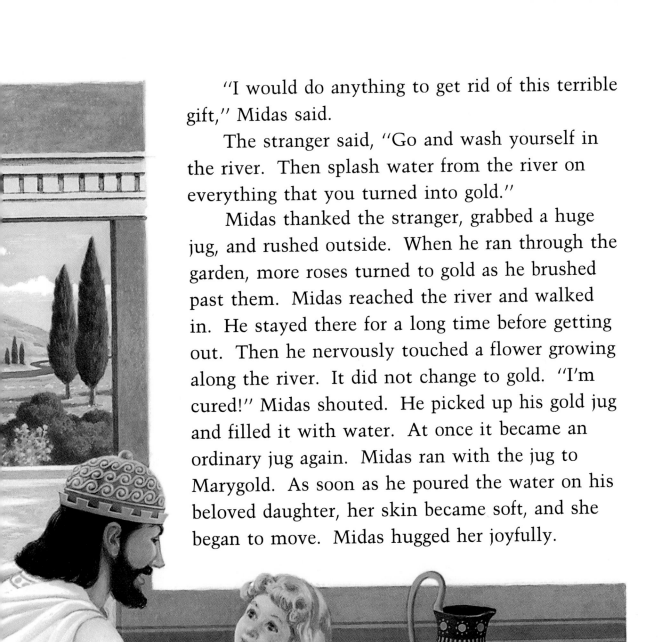

Midas and Marygold went through the house and the garden. They splashed water from the river on everything Midas had turned into gold. They didn't leave out even one rose.

After what seemed like a very long time, Midas woke up. He realized that everything that he thought had happened was only a dream. Midas' dream had taught him an important lesson. His love for his daughter was more important than all the gold in the world.

Many, many years later, when Midas was a grandfather, he would hold Marygold's children on his knees and tell them about his dream, very much the way I've told it to you. When he finished, he would stroke the children's golden curls. Then he would tell them that the gold in their hair was the only gold he valued.

Reader's Response ～ Have you ever had a wish come true, only to be disappointed?

All That Glitters: Facts About Gold

Gold has been called the metal that lives forever. It never loses its color, it can be melted down and used again and again, and it doesn't rust.

An ounce of gold is about the size of a fifty-cent coin. One ounce can be hammered into a sheet larger than a living room rug.

The world's first gold coins are often said to have been made by a king named Croesus over two thousand years ago. Have you ever heard the expression, "Rich as Croesus"?

Gold's properties are well suited for high-technology use; the precious metal is used in making spacecrafts, video cameras, cellular phones, computers, and calculators.

117

I'll Tell You a Story

I'll tell you a story
About Jack a Nory,
And now my story's begun;

I'll tell you another
Of Jack and his brother,
And now my story is done.

Mother Goose

Reading

A story is a special thing.
The ones that I have read,
They do not stay inside the books.
They stay inside my head.

Marchette Chute

There was an old pig with a pen
Who wrote stories and verse now and then.
To enhance these creations,
He drew illustrations
With brushes, some paints and his pen.

written and illustrated by Arnold Lobel
from The Book of Pigericks

The Emperor's Plum Tree

written and illustrated by Michelle Nikly
translated by Elizabeth Shub

Long ago, in the land of the rising sun, there lived an emperor whose garden was beautiful beyond imagination. Each tree, each flower, each stone had its place in the total harmony of the design.

One morning as the emperor took his daily stroll, he stopped in dismay at a grove of plum trees. Could that tree near the wall be dying? He hurried to it. He felt a twig. It broke off in his hand, brittle and dry. The tree would have to be cut down. The perfect garden would be perfect no longer. The emperor shut himself up in his palace and refused to go out.

Days passed, and indoors, the emperor mourned his garden. At last it was decided that only a plum tree as beautiful as the one that died could restore the garden and make the emperor happy again. Messengers were sent to search the land and within a day a perfect tree was found in the garden of a painter named Ukiyo.

Ukiyo, his wife Tanka, and their small son Musuko were desolate when they learned that their tree had been chosen for the imperial garden. Ukiyo loved to paint its gnarled branches and starlike flowers, and many of the poems Tanka wrote described its beauty.

But most of all, the plum tree was the home of Musuko's friend, the nightingale. Musuko often stood at the foot of the tree and spoke to her. She replied in her own way, yet they always understood one another as true friends do.

Ukiyo knew they had to part with the tree, but he asked if they might keep it one day longer.

When the plum tree was about to be taken away, Musuko approached the emperor's messenger. He asked if he might tie a scroll to one of its branches. The messenger, seeing how bravely the boy choked back his tears, lifted him up so that he could attach the scroll.

The plum tree was replanted in the imperial garden and the emperor was persuaded to come and see it. He gazed at it while the courtiers waited anxiously. At last, to everyone's relief, he smiled. The emperor's garden was flawless once again.

Then the emperor noticed Musuko's scroll. He took it down and unrolled it.

What he saw was a wonderfully lifelike drawing of a branch of the plum tree, and perched on the branch was a nightingale. Beneath the painting was a poem.

> At the long day's end,
> when the nightingale flies home,
> what shall I tell her?

 or a long
time, the emperor stood in thought before the plum tree.
Then he sent a messenger to bring Ukiyo, Tanka, and
Musuko to the palace. The following day, they
appeared before him. He spoke first to Musuko.

"My child," the emperor said, "I will tell you
what to say to your homeless friend. Tell her that her
plum tree, borrowed for a day because of the emperor's
whim, will be returned to her by the emperor's order."

Ukiyo and Tanka were about to protest, but the
emperor would not let them.

"It seems that my sorrow has been replaced by yours. I could not bear to see this tree each day, knowing that a child lost his friend because of me. This tree belongs in your garden, but before it leaves mine, I have a request. Ukiyo, I ask you to paint my garden, perfect as it is on this day.

"The death of my plum tree has reminded me that no garden can last forever. One day the peach trees, the pines, and even the bamboos will be no more. But your painting, Ukiyo, will be a lasting reminder of this garden's perfection.

"And, Tanka, I ask you to write this story, just as it happened, so that in times to come children will hear how once the Emperor of Japan learned wisdom from a small boy named Musuko, a nightingale, and a plum tree."

Reader's Response ～ What was your favorite part of this story? What made you like it best?

A Perfect Garden,
A Perfect Gift

Every spring vacation, thousands of schoolchildren visit Washington, D.C. Among the wonderful things to see in the nation's capital in spring are the cherry blossoms—a perfect garden. The flowers look like pink and white clouds floating through the city. Where did these cherry blossoms come from?

In 1912, the city of Tokyo gave Washington, D.C., 3,000 cherry trees as a gift of friendship. William Howard Taft was president then. His wife planted the first tree.

Years later when Japan's cherry trees began to die, the United States had a chance to repay Tokyo for its lovely gift. Cuttings were taken from our trees to send back to Japan.

Can you think of a better gift?

127

128

Sam,
Bangs &
Moonshine

written and illustrated by Evaline Ness

On a small island, near a large harbor, there once lived a fisherman's little daughter (named Samantha, but always called Sam), who had the reckless habit of lying.

Not even the sailors home from the sea could tell stranger stories than Sam. Not even the ships in the harbor, with curious cargoes from giraffes to gerbils, claimed more wonders than Sam did.

Sam said her mother was a mermaid, when everyone knew she was dead.

Sam said she had a fierce lion at home, and a baby kangaroo. (Actually, what she *really* had was an old wise cat called Bangs.)

Sam even said that Bangs could talk if and when he wanted to.

Sam said this. Sam said that. But whatever Sam said you could never believe.

Even Bangs yawned and shook his head when she said the ragged old rug on the doorstep was a chariot drawn by dragons.

Early one morning, before Sam's father left in his fishing boat to be gone all day, he hugged Sam hard and said, "Today, for a change, talk REAL not MOONSHINE. MOONSHINE spells trouble."

Sam promised. But while she washed the dishes, made the beds, and swept the floor, she wondered what he meant. When she asked Bangs to explain REAL and MOONSHINE, Bangs jumped on her shoulder and purred, "MOONSHINE is flummadiddle. REAL is the opposite."

Sam decided that Bangs made no sense whatever.

When the sun made a golden star on the cracked window, Sam knew it was time to expect Thomas.

Thomas lived in the tall grand house on the hill. Thomas had two cows in the barn, twenty-five sheep, a bicycle with a basket, and a jungle-gym on the lawn. But most important of all, Thomas believed every word Sam said.

At the same time every day Thomas rode his bicycle down the hill to Sam's house and begged to see her baby kangaroo.

Every day Sam told Thomas it had just "stepped out." She sent Thomas everywhere to find it. She sent him to the tallest trees where, she said, it was visiting owls. Or perhaps it was up in the old windmill, grinding corn for its evening meal.

"It might be," said Sam, "in the lighthouse tower, warning ships at sea."

"Or maybe," she said, "it's asleep on the sand. Somewhere, anywhere on the beach."

Wherever Sam sent Thomas, he went. He climbed up trees, ran down steps, and scoured the beach, but he never found Sam's baby kangaroo.

While Thomas searched, Sam sat in her chariot and was drawn by dragons to faraway secret worlds.

Today, when Thomas arrived, Sam said, "That baby kangaroo just left to visit my mermaid mother. She lives in a cave behind Blue Rock."

Sam watched Thomas race away on his bicycle over the narrow strand that stretched to a massive blue rock in the distance. Then she sat down in her chariot. Bangs came out of the house and sat down beside Sam. With his head turned in the direction of the diminishing Thomas, Bangs said, "When the tide comes up, it covers the road to Blue Rock. Tide rises early today."

Sam looked at Bangs for a minute. Then she said, "Pardon me while I go to the moon."

Bangs stood up. He stretched his front legs. Then he stretched his back legs. Slowly he stalked away from Sam toward Blue Rock.

Suddenly Sam had no desire to go to the moon. Or any other place either. She just sat in her chariot and thought about Bangs and Thomas.

She was so busy thinking that she was unaware of thick muddy clouds that blocked out the sun. Nor did she hear the menacing rumble of thunder. She was almost knocked off the doorstep when a sudden gust of wind drove torrents of rain against her face.

Sam leaped into the house and slammed the door. She went to the window to look at Blue Rock, but she could see nothing through the grey ribbed curtain of rain. She wondered where Thomas was. She wondered where Bangs was. Sam stood there looking at nothing, trying to swallow the lump that rose in her throat.

The murky light in the room deepened to black. Sam was still at the window when her father burst into the house. Water streamed from his hat and oozed from his boots. Sam ran to him screaming, "Bangs and Thomas are out on the rock! Blue Rock! Bangs and Thomas!"

As her father turned quickly and ran out the door, he ordered Sam to stay in the house.

"And pray that the tide hasn't covered the rock!" he yelled.

When her father had gone, Sam sat down. She listened to the rain hammer on the tin roof. Then suddenly it stopped. Sam closed her eyes and mouth, tight. She waited in the quiet room. It seemed to her that she waited forever.

At last she heard her father's footsteps outside. She flung open the door and said one word: "Bangs?"

Sam's father shook his head.

"He was washed away," he said. "But I found Thomas on the rock. I brought him back in the boat. He's home now, safe in bed. Can you tell me how all this happened?"

Sam started to explain, but sobs choked her. She cried so hard that it was a long time before her father understood everything.

Finally, Sam's father said, "Go to bed now. But before you go to sleep, Sam, tell yourself the difference between REAL and MOONSHINE."

Sam went to her room and crept into bed. With her eyes wide open she thought about REAL and MOONSHINE.

MOONSHINE was a mermaid-mother, a fierce lion, a chariot drawn by dragons, and certainly a baby kangaroo. It was all flummadiddle just as Bangs had told her. Or *had* he told her? Wouldn't her father say that a cat's talking was MOONSHINE?

REAL was no mother at all. REAL was her father and Bangs. And now there wasn't even Bangs. Tears welled up in Sam's eyes again. They ran down into her ears making a scratching noise. Sam sat up and blew her nose. The scratching was not in her ears. It was at the window. As Sam stared at the black oblong, two enormous yellow eyes appeared and stared back. Sam sprang from her bed and opened the window. There sat Bangs, his coat a sodden mess.

"Oh, Bangs!" cried Sam, as she grabbed and smothered him with kisses. "What happened to you?"

In a few words Bangs told her that one moment he was on the rock with Thomas and the next he was lying at the foot of the lighthouse tower a mile away. All done by waves.

"Nasty stuff, water," Bangs grumbled, as he washed himself from his ears to his feet.

Sam patted Bangs. "Well, at least it's not flummadiddle. . . ." Sam paused. She looked up to see her father standing in the doorway.

"Look! Bangs is home!" shouted Sam.

"Hello, Bangs. What's not flummadiddle?" asked Sam's father.

"Bangs! And you! And Thomas!" answered Sam. "Oh, Daddy! I'll always know the difference between REAL and MOONSHINE now. Bangs and Thomas were almost lost because of MOONSHINE. Bangs told me."

"He *told* you?" questioned Sam's father.

"Well, he would have *if* he could talk," said Sam. Then she added sadly, "I know cats can't talk like people, but I almost believed I *did* have a baby kangaroo."

Her father looked steadily at her.

"There's good MOONSHINE and bad MOON-SHINE," he said. "The important thing is to know the difference." He kissed Sam good night and left the room.

When he had closed the door, Sam said, "You know, Bangs, I might just keep my chariot."

This time Bangs did not yawn and shake his head. Instead he licked her hand. He waited until she got into bed, then he curled up at her feet and went to sleep.

139

The next morning Sam opened her eyes to see an incredible thing! Hopping toward her on its hind legs was a small, elegant, large-eyed animal with a long tail like a lion's. Behind it strolled Bangs and her father.

"A baby kangaroo!" shouted Sam. "Where did you find it!"

"It is *not* a baby kangaroo," said Sam's father. "It's a gerbil. I found it on an African banana boat in the harbor."

"Now Thomas can see a baby kangaroo at last!" Sam squealed with joy.

Sam's father interrupted her. "Stop the MOONSHINE, Sam. Call it by its REAL name. Anyway, Thomas won't come today. He's sick in bed with laryngitis. He can't even talk. Also his bicycle got lost in the storm."

Sam looked down at the gerbil. Gently she stroked its tiny head. Without raising her eyes, she said, "Daddy, do you think I should *give* the gerbil to Thomas?"

Sam's father said nothing. Bangs licked his tail.

Suddenly Sam hollered, "Come on, Bangs!"

She jumped out of bed and slipped into her shoes. As she grabbed her coat, she picked up the gerbil, and ran from the house with Bangs at her heels. Sam did not stop running until she stood at the side of Thomas's bed.

Very carefully she placed the gerbil on Thomas's stomach. The little animal sat straight up on its long hind legs and gazed directly at Thomas with its immense round eyes.

"Whaaaaaaaaaa sis name!" wheezed Thomas.

"MOONSHINE," answered Sam, as she gave Bangs a big wide smile.

Reader's Response ∾ Would you like to have Sam for a friend? Why or why not?

Working It Out

The world is full of puzzles and problems.

How do people work out their own solutions?

HAVING A BALL, *multimedia sculpture by George Rhoads, American, 1984*

Working It Out

Sometimes it takes creative thinking to solve your problems. And often you have to try more than once. The characters in these stories use their heads—and hearts—to solve their problems.

❋ In *The Tale of the Mandarin Ducks* by Katherine Paterson, a cruel lord captures a beautiful duck but leaves the duck's plainer mate behind. When two kind servants risk their lives to reunite the mandarin ducks, there is trouble ahead.

144

✳ Bimwili certainly has a mind of her own in *Bimwili & the Zimwi* by Verna Aardema. While at the sea with her sisters, she wanders off alone and is captured by an ugly creature called a Zimwi. How can she escape?

More Books to Enjoy

The Major and the Mousehole Mice
by Jane Chelsea Aragon
The Many Lives of Benjamin Franklin by Aliki
Seven Kisses in a Row by Patricia MacLachlan
Something Queer at the Library by Elizabeth Levy

Sybil Rides
FOR INDEPENDENCE

by Drollene P. Brown

It was the year 1777. The American colonists were fighting to win their independence from Great Britain. On the night of April 26, 1777, a man on horseback came to the home of Colonel Ludington to tell him the British were burning the nearby town of Danbury. The rider was too tired to go on. Yet someone had to warn the American soldiers. Sybil, the colonel's sixteen-year-old daughter, said she would do it. Sybil and her horse Star would have to ride all night.

Sybil swung up on Star.
She patted his neck and leaned toward his ear.
"This ride is for freedom," she whispered.

The colonel looked up at his daughter.
He handed her a big stick.
"Listen for others on the path," he warned.
"Pull off and hide if you hear hoofbeats
or footsteps or voices.

"You know where to go.
Tell our men that Danbury's burning.
Tell them to gather at Ludingtons'."
Sybil listened to her orders.
She saluted her father, her colonel.
He stepped back and returned the salute.

Sybil thought of what might happen.
There were more than thirty miles to cover
in the dark and rain.
She could be lost or hurt or caught by Redcoats!
But she did not let these black thoughts scare her.
I will do it for the colonies, she vowed.

She turned Star south on a line with the river.
There would be several lone farmhouses to alert
before they reached Shaw's Pond.

It was almost eight o'clock
when she reached the first farmhouse.
Doors flew open at the sound of Star's hoofbeats.

Sybil shouted her message. She did not stop,
but hurried on to the farmhouses
along Horse Pound Road.

It was about ten o'clock
when Sybil reached Shaw's Pond.
The houses beside the water
were dark for the night.

Sybil hadn't thought of this.
She had been so excited
she had forgotten people would be sleeping.

Sybil stopped for only a moment.
She coaxed Star up to the door
and pounded with her stick.

A window opened.
A head poked out.
"Look to the east!" Sybil shouted.
"Danbury's burning! Gather at Ludingtons'!"

She did not beat on every door.
She did not shout at every house.
Neighbors called to each other;
and in the little hamlets along her way,
one of the first ones awakened
rushed out to ring the town bell.

When the alarm began to sound,
Sybil would stop her shouting
and ride on into the darkness.

Her throat hurt from calling out her message.
Her heart beat wildly, and her tired eyes burned.
Her skirt seemed to be filled with heavy weights,
for it was wet and caked with mud.
She pulled her mother's cloak closer
against the cold and rain that would not stop.

Sybil would not stop, either.
All the men in the regiment must be told.
She urged Star on.

Outside the village at Mahopac Pond,
Star slipped in the mud.
He got up right away,
but Sybil's eyes stung with tears.
She would have to be more careful!

If Star were hurt, she would blame herself.
She must walk Star over loose rocks
and pick through the underbrush
where there was no path.

Again and again, Sybil woke up sleeping soldiers.
Nearing Red Mills, Star stumbled and almost fell.
He was breathing heavily.
"You are fine, Star," Sybil whispered.

Sybil looked at the sky.
The moon was half-risen.
That meant it was well past midnight.
She guessed they were halfway through,
but the long ride to Stormville still lay ahead.

More slowly now, they started on their way.
Then—hoofbeats on the path!
Quickly Sybil reined Star to a halt.
She jumped down and pulled him toward the trees.

She held her breath and strained her eyes.
Men passed so close she could have touched them.
They looked like British soldiers,
but sometimes skinners dressed like soldiers
of one army or the other
to fool the people they robbed.

Soon the hoofbeats died away.
Sybil's hands and knees trembled
as she guided Star back to the path.
"We'll make it," she softly promised him.
Star pricked up his ears and started off again.
He was weary, but he trusted Sybil.

When they reached Stormville,
the alarm had already begun to sound.
Someone from another village had come with the news.
Sybil was glad, for she could only whisper.
She had shouted away her voice.

Covered with mud,
Horse and rider turned home.

When Sybil rode into her yard,
more than four hundred men were ready to march.
She looked at the eastern sky.
It was red.

"Is Danbury still burning?" she asked
and tumbled into Father's arms.

"No, my brave soldier.
It is the sunrise.
You have ridden all night."

"I do not feel like a brave soldier," Sybil whispered.
"I feel like a very tired girl.
Star needs care," she murmured sleepily
as she was carried to her bed.

Early that morning,
while that very tired girl slept,
her father's men joined soldiers from Connecticut.
They met the British at Ridgefield,
about ten miles from Danbury.

The soldiers from New York and Connecticut
battled with the Redcoats.
Most of the British escaped to their ships
in Long Island Sound,
but they did no further damage.

People spread the word of Sybil's ride.
Soon General Washington came to her house
to thank her for her courage.
Statesman Alexander Hamilton wrote to her,
praising her deed.

America was soon a growing, changing nation,
and Sybil's life changed, too.
At twenty-three she married Edmond Ogden.
They had six children, and she kept house.
She baked, she mended, and she washed the dishes.

But sometimes she would stop
in the middle of a chore.
Remembering that cold, wet night in 1777,
she would shiver again.
Then warm feelings of pride would fill her
as she thought, "Once I was brave for my country."

Sybil lived to be seventy-eight years old.
Her children and her children's children
loved to hear the story
of a young girl's ride for independence.

Reader's Response ∾ What qualities of
Sybil's do you admire?

For Love of Country

What do these women have in common? Each of them played a courageous role in American history.

Lydia Darragh

During the Revolutionary War, British officers met at the home of Lydia Darragh in Philadelphia. She overheard the officers planning an attack on the American soldiers at nearby Whitemarsh. Lydia smuggled a warning past British troops. General Washington used Lydia's information to prepare for the "secret" attack, and the British attempt failed.

Sacagawea

In 1805 and 1806, Sacagawea, a young Shoshoni woman, traveled with Lewis and Clark as they explored the West. Sacagawea was their helper and interpreter. She found edible plants and got horses for the expedition from Indians the party met during the long and difficult journey. She helped the explorers to reach the Pacific Ocean and return safely home.

Harriet Tubman

Harriet Tubman was an escaped slave who worked on the Underground Railroad in the years before the Civil War. She made nineteen dangerous trips south to lead other escaped slaves to freedom. She was so successful that slave owners offered a $40,000 reward for her, but she was never caught.

8,000 STONES

A Chinese Folktale

told by Diane Wolkstein
illustrated by Ed Young

¹ Long ago in China, there lived a very powerful ruler. ² He was known as the Most Supreme Governor of China. ³ His name was Ts'ao Ts'ao.

⁴ Ts'ao Ts'ao ruled the royal city of Loyang and lived in a beautiful palace surrounded by lovely gardens. ⁵ The treasures of the royal city and palace were well protected by the Governor's mighty army of 10,000 soldiers.

⁶ But the neighboring kings and princes heard of Ts'ao Ts'ao's beautiful palace and mighty army, and they came themselves or sent messengers to see the wonders of the royal city.

⁷ The messengers often brought splendid presents.

This year the Satrap, or prince, of India sent Ts'ao Ts'ao a most unusual present: a present that neither Ts'ao Ts'ao nor anyone in Ts'ao Ts'ao's kingdom had ever seen before. When the Indian messengers arrived in Loyang, the peasants came running from their fields to see the marvelous creature. The courtiers came out of the palace, and soon a huge noisy crowd formed around the animal.

Then Ts'ao Ts'ao appeared, and the Indian messengers, the peasants, and all the court knelt before him.

"Rise!" Ts'ao Ts'ao commanded the Indian messengers. "Rise and explain the cause of this uproar. What is this beast doing in my kingdom?"

"It is a present," explained the messengers. "It is a present from the Grand Satrap of India to the Most Supreme Governor of China, Ruler of Loyang, General of 10,000 soldiers—Yourself!"

"Oh . . . oh yes," muttered Ts'ao Ts'ao. (He just then remembered that this was the time of year the Satrap's presents usually did arrive.)

"Delighted!" exclaimed Ts'ao Ts'ao. "The Grand Satrap of India is to be informed that I am delighted with his . . . his . . . what is it called, his . . . ?"

158

"Elephant!" answered the messengers. Junma, the son of one of the Indian messengers, showed his small ivory elephant to P'ei, the son of Ts'ao Ts'ao. P'ei showed Junma his new Chinese sailboat.

"And how tall is my elephant?" asked Ts'ao Ts'ao.

"Ten feet tall, Most Supreme Governor of China."

"And how much does my elephant weigh?"

"Oh, we cannot tell you Most Supreme Governor. There are no scales in India large enough to weigh such an animal."

"You mean to say that the Grand Satrap of India does not know how much an elephant weighs?"

"That is correct, Most Supreme Governor of China."

"I see," said Ts'ao Ts'ao, "I see. . . ."

When the Indian messengers had been led into the palace to eat and rest, Ts'ao Ts'ao called his advisers together: "I want to know, before the messengers leave at the end of the month, the exact weight of my elephant. If the Grand Satrap of India does not know how to weigh an elephant, then I, Ts'ao Ts'ao, Ruler of Loyang, General of 10,000 soldiers, shall show him the way!"

The advisers then spent all their time thinking: How to weigh an elephant . . . ? How to weigh the Most Supreme Governor of China's elephant? How to weigh the elephant? But they could not think of a way. Then a week before the messengers were to leave, little P'ei came from playing with his sailboat to see the wonderful elephant.

"What are you doing under the elephant?" he called to the advisers.

"Shhh . . . we're thinking."

"What about?" whispered P'ei.

"How to weigh an elephant," the advisers whispered back.

"Well, that's not so hard," said P'ei.

"Not so hard?" cried the advisers.

"No," said P'ei. "Follow me, and I'll show you."

P'ei led them through the woods to a small pond near the palace. There by the pond was P'ei's new toy sailboat. It looked like any toy Chinese sailboat, except it had a strange line carved into its side.

"Wait here!" cried P'ei and he ran back to the palace.

The advisers picked up the boat. They examined the line carefully. At the side of the line was the Chinese character for elephant.

What did it mean?

The advisers shook their heads.

They did not understand.

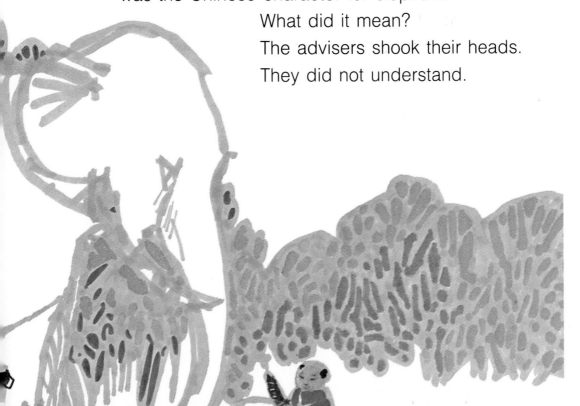

Little P'ei returned from the palace, carrying Junma's ivory elephant.

"Watch," he said to the advisers.

He placed the elephant on the sailboat and the boat sank in the water to the carved line.

"You see," P'ei explained, "no matter how many times I sailed Junma's elephant on my boat, it always weighed the boat down to that line, so I carved his character next to it. If you want to weigh the big elephant, you can do the same thing. And if you need to know the exact weight of the elephant, then pile stones on the boat until the boat sinks to the elephant's character."

"That's it! That's it!" cried the advisers. "Little P'ei, you've shown us the way."

On the day of the weighing, a large crowd of courtiers and peasants gathered around the shore of the palace lake.

The elephant was led from the fields onto a sturdy barge. Little P'ei and the advisers then stepped into a smaller boat.

Little P'ei was given the honor of carving, just above the water line, the character of the Most Supreme Governor of China's elephant on the barge.

After both boats were brought back to shore, the barge was pushed out again. Many stones were piled on it. It took many, many stones for the barge to sink to the character of the elephant. Can you guess how much the elephant weighed?

The elephant weighed 8000 stones.

A gong was sounded and the announcement made by the court herald:

"The Most Supreme Governor of China's elephant weighs the Most High Amount of 8000 stones!"

The peasants cheered and the courtiers applauded. The gong rang out again. This time Ts'ao Ts'ao, Most Supreme Governor of China, Ruler of Loyang, General of 10,000 soldiers, spoke:

"Let it be known that the plan for the weighing of the Most Supreme Governor of China's elephant was thought of by none other than my own son . . . little P'ei."

The peasants, the advisers, and the courtiers cheered even louder.

"AND let it be written in the court annals," continued Ts'ao Ts'ao, "and a copy be given to the Indian messengers to present to the Grand Satrap of India."

So the story of little P'ei and the weight of the elephant was written out and presented to the Indian messengers to take back to the Satrap.

And Ts'ao Ts'ao, Most Supreme Governor of China, then became famous—not only for his beautiful palace and mighty army—but also for the Most Supreme Intelligence of his clever son . . . little P'ei.

In later years, little P'ei became Ts'ao P'ei, EMPEROR OF ALL OF CHINA. That was in A.D. 200, almost 2000 years ago.

Reader's Response ∾ What part of this story did you most enjoy?

A SHORT HISTORY OF NUMBERS

■ Early people used ten fingers to show "how many." Today our number system is still based on tens.

■ People in Egypt and Mesopotamia were writing real numbers as long as 5,000 years ago. Some ancient people used a counting board like the abacus that is still used today in China, Japan, and other countries.

■ Ancient Greeks gave names to their numbers. Today, Greek number names are hidden in English words. *Tri* comes from the Greek word for three. How many wheels does a tricycle have? How many sides are in a triangle?

■ Romans invented a new way of writing numbers. One was I; five was V; ten was X. Today some clocks have Roman numerals on their faces. Often dates on buildings or statues are written in Roman numerals.

■ Beginning in the 700s A.D., the Arabs adapted the number symbols of the Hindus into the form we use today. We call 0, 1, 2, 3, 4, 5, 6, 7, 8, and 9 Arabic, or Hindu-Arabic, numerals.

Brother Eagle, Sister Sky

Paintings by Susan Jeffers

In a time so long ago that nearly all traces of it are lost in the prairie dust, an ancient people were a part of the land that we love and call America. Living here for thousands of years, their children became the great Indian civilizations of the Choctaw and Cherokee, Navaho, Iroquois and Sioux, among many others. Then white settlers from Europe began a bloody war against the Indians, and in the span of a single lifetime claimed all the Indians' land for themselves, allowing them only small tracts of land to live on.

When the last of the Indian wars were drawing to a close, one of the bravest and most respected chiefs of the Northwest Nations, Chief Seattle, sat at a white man's table to sign a paper presented by the new Commissioner of Indian Affairs for the Territory. The government in Washington, D.C., wished to buy the lands of Chief Seattle's people.

With a commanding presence and eyes that mirrored the great soul that lived within, the Chief rose to speak to the gathering in a resounding voice.

How can you buy the sky? Chief Seattle began.
How can you own the rain and the wind?

My mother told me,
Every part of this earth is sacred to
our people.
Every pine needle. Every sandy shore.
Every mist in the dark woods.
Every meadow and humming insect.
All are holy in the memory of our people.

169

My father said to me,
I know the sap that courses through the trees
as I know the blood that flows in my veins.
We are part of the earth and it is part of us.
The perfumed flowers are our sisters.

170

The bear, the deer, the great eagle, these are our brothers.
The rocky crests, the meadows,
the ponies—all belong to the same family.   173

The voice of my ancestors said to me,
The shining water that moves in the streams and rivers is
not simply water, but the blood of your grandfather's grandfather.
Each ghostly reflection in the clear waters of the lakes tells
of memories in the life of our people.
The water's murmur is the voice of your great-great-grandmother.
The rivers are our brothers. They quench our thirst.
They carry our canoes and feed our children.
You must give to the rivers the kindness you would give
to any brother.

The voice of my grandfather said to me,
The air is precious. It shares its spirit with all
the life it supports. The wind that gave me my first
breath also received my last sigh.
You must keep the land and air apart and sacred,
as a place where one can go to taste the wind that
is sweetened by the meadow flowers.

When the last Red Man and Woman have vanished with
their wilderness, and their memory is only the shadow of a
cloud moving across the prairie, will the shores and forest
still be here?

Will there be any of the spirit of my people left?

My ancestors said to me, This we know:

The earth does not belong to us. We belong to the earth.

The voice of my grandmother said to me,
Teach your children what you have been taught.
The earth is our mother.
What befalls the earth befalls all the sons and daughters
of the earth.

Hear my voice and the voice of my ancestors,
Chief Seattle said.
The destiny of your people is a mystery to us.
What will happen when the buffalo are all slaughtered?
The wild horses tamed?
What will happen when the secret corners of the forest are
heavy with the scent of many men?

When the view of the ripe hills is blotted by
talking wires?
Where will the thicket be? Gone.
Where will the eagle be? Gone!
And what will happen when we say good-bye to the
swift pony and the hunt?
It will be the end of living, and the beginning of survival.

This we know: All things are connected like the blood
that unites us.
We did not weave the web of life,
We are merely a strand in it.
Whatever we do to the web, we do to ourselves.

We love this earth as a newborn loves its mother's
heartbeat.
If we sell you our land, care for it as we have
cared for it.
Hold in your mind the memory of the land as it
is when you receive it.
Preserve the land and the air and the rivers for your
children's children and love it as we have loved it.

Reader's Response ～ If you could meet
with Chief Seattle, what would you ask him?

Chief Seattle

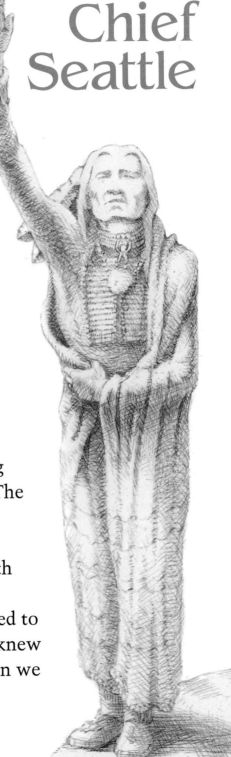

One of America's best known cities was named for Chief Sealth, called Chief Seattle by white settlers.

When the first white settlers came to Puget Sound, Chief Seattle urged his people to welcome them. The new settlement was first known as Duwamps, but soon people wanted a new name for their village.

Dr. David Maynard, a physician who was a friend of Chief Seattle, suggested naming the settlement after the chief. The villagers agreed.

When Chief Seattle died in 1866, hundreds of admirers, both Indian and white, came to the funeral. Another chief is reported to have spoken these words: "He knew better what was good for us than we knew ourselves."

Fidelia

by Gary Apple
based on the story
by Ruth Adams

Characters:

Miss Toomey
Alberto
Fidelia
Trombone players
Clarinet players
Carpenter
Papa Julio
Carmela
Drum players
Violin players
Shopkeeper
Mrs. Reed

Miss Toomey: (*to the audience*) Hello. My name is Miss Toomey. I conduct the school orchestra. Today, I'm going to tell you a story about the most interesting orchestra member I ever had. Her name is Fidelia Ortega! Fidelia came from a very musical family. Her father, Papa Julio, played the trumpet.

(Papa Julio *enters playing the trumpet.*)

Papa Julio: *Ta-ra-rar-ta! Ta-ra-rar-ta! Ta-ra-rar-ta!*

Miss Toomey: Fidelia's older brother, Alberto, was in my orchestra, too. He played the slide trombone.

(Alberto *enters playing his trombone.*)

Alberto: *Toom-room-room-room! Toom-room-room-room! Room-toom-room!*

Miss Toomey: Carmela, Fidelia's older sister, was also in my orchestra. She played the clarinet.

(Carmela *enters playing the clarinet.*)

Carmela: *Tootle-tee! Tootle-tee! Tootle-tum-tee!*

Miss Toomey: Yes, the Ortegas were a very musical family, except for little Fidelia. She didn't play a musical instrument.

(Fidelia *enters looking sad.*)

Fidelia: I want to make music too, Papa.

Papa Julio: You are too little, Fidelia. You will have to wait until you grow a little more.

Fidelia: But I don't want to wait!

Alberto: You can't play a trombone. (*He plays.*) *Toom-room-room!* Your arms are too short to work the slide.

Carmela: You can't play a clarinet. (*She plays.*) *Tootle-tee-tee!* You need all of your front teeth to play the clarinet.

Fidelia: I don't want to play a trombone or a clarinet. I want to play the violin!

Alberto: A violin? Don't be silly. Your arms are too short. Your hands are too small.

Carmela: You could not draw the bow or hold the strings down tight.

Papa Julio: They're right, Fidelia. Besides, you have to be in the fourth grade to play the violin in Miss Toomey's orchestra. I'm afraid you'll just have to wait.

ACT TWO

Miss Toomey: (*to the audience*) But Fidelia wanted to play the violin so badly, she could not wait. One day, she sneaked into the band room while my orchestra was practicing.

Drum Players: *Bump-be-dump! Bump-be-dump!*

Alberto and Other Trombone Players: *Toom-room-room-room. Toom-room-room!*

Violin Players: *Tink-plink-tunk! Tink-plink-tunk!*

Carmela and Other Clarinet Players: *Tootle-tee! Tootle-tu! Tootle-tee!*

Miss Toomey: (*to the audience*) Suddenly, our practicing came to a stop when we heard a loud CRASH!

(*A loud noise is heard.*)

Fidelia: Sorry. I tripped over the drums.

Carmela: Oh, no!

Alberto: Miss Toomey, this is my sister Fidelia.

Miss Toomey: (*to* Fidelia) Hello, Fidelia. What were you doing hiding behind the drums?

Fidelia: I want to play in your orchestra.

Miss Toomey: Do you, now? You're very young. What instrument do you want to play?

Fidelia: The violin!

Miss Toomey: Dear me, I'm afraid you are too small to play the violin, and it is very difficult to play. I'm sorry.

(Fidelia *sadly turns to leave.*)

Wait, Fidelia. I need a tom-tom player for the Indian dance we are learning. Would you like to play the tom-tom?

Fidelia: (*happy*) Oh, yes!

ACT THREE

Miss Toomey: (*to the audience*) And that's how Fidelia joined my orchestra. Fidelia enjoyed playing the tom-tom, but every week she would ask the same question.

Fidelia: (*to* Miss Toomey) Have I grown enough to play the violin yet?

Miss Toomey: (*to* Fidelia) No, not yet, Fidelia. (*to the audience*) Then, one day, I had some very important news to tell my orchestra. (*to the orchestra*) Boys and girls, Mrs. Reed, the director of the All City Orchestra, will be visiting us next week. She will choose the best musicians to be part of the All City Orchestra, so you must practice very hard.

Fidelia: I want to play for Mrs. Reed, too.

Alberto: But, Fidelia, you can't play a tune on the tom-tom.

Fidelia: Then I'll play a tune on something else!

(Fidelia *runs from the room.*)

ACT FOUR

Miss Toomey: (*to the audience*) Fidelia had a plan. On her way home, she stopped by a gift shop.

(Fidelia *enters the gift shop. A shopkeeper is unpacking a vase from a wooden box.*)

Shopkeeper: Can I help you, young lady?

Fidelia: Yes, I'd like to buy that box.

Shopkeeper: This box? You don't have to buy it. I will give it to you.

(*The* shopkeeper *gives her the box.*)

Fidelia: Oh, thank you!

Miss Toomey: (*to the audience*) Next, Fidelia stopped by a carpenter who was building a fence.

Fidelia: Excuse me. Might you have a small piece of wood that you can give me?

Carpenter: Sure, I have lots of wood pieces that I don't need. (*He hands her a piece of wood.*)

Fidelia: This will work fine. Thanks!

ACT FIVE

Miss Toomey: (*to the audience*) Fidelia ran home. She went into the garage, where she found a hammer and some nails. She tried to nail the board to the box, but had some trouble.

(Fidelia *hits her thumb with the hammer.*)

Fidelia: Ouch!

(Carmela *and* Alberto *enter.*)

Alberto: What are you doing in here?

Fidelia: I'm making something.

Carmela: What is it?

Fidelia: Do you promise not to laugh?

Alberto and Carmela: We promise.

Fidelia: I'm making a violin. But I can't get the nails to go in straight.

Alberto: Here, let us help.

Miss Toomey: (*to the audience*) Alberto and Carmela helped Fidelia build her homemade violin. It had nails for pegs, rubber bands for strings, and a clothespin for a bridge that the strings would go over.

Alberto: There, we're finished!

Carmela: Let's hear how it sounds.

Fidelia: OK, here I go. (*She plays her violin.*) *Twang-buzz-twank-thup.*

Carmela: (*She covers her ears.*) It sounds awful!

Fidelia: Maybe if I tighten the rubber bands it will sound better. (*She tightens them and plays again.*) *Zing-zong-zunk-zunk.*

Alberto: Well, it's better. But it still sounds pretty terrible.

Fidelia: I just have to practice a little more. (*She plays.*) *Zing-twang-zong-twang . . .*

Carmela: I can't stand it. I'm getting out of here. (*She leaves.*)

Alberto: Me, too. (*He leaves.*)

Fidelia: (*to herself*) It doesn't sound so bad to me. (*She begins to practice some more.*) *Twang-boing-zang-zang.*

ACT SIX

Miss Toomey: (*to the audience*) Fidelia practiced and practiced and practiced. Finally, the day for the All City Orchestra tryouts had come. (*to the orchestra members*) Children, I'd like you all to meet Mrs. Reed, the director of the All City Orchestra.

Mrs. Reed: Hello, students.

Orchestra Members: Hello, Mrs. Reed.

Miss Toomey: (*to* Mrs. Reed) Mrs. Reed, to start with, the orchestra would like to play "The Man on the Flying Trapeze."

Mrs. Reed: Wonderful. I love that melody.

Miss Toomey: (*She waves her baton.*) Ready? Begin.

(*At the same time, the musicians play "The Man on the Flying Trapeze." All of a sudden, a strange sound comes from the back of the orchestra. It's* Fidelia *playing her homemade violin.*)

Fidelia: (*She plays.*) *Buzz-zang-zong-zong-zing!*

Miss Toomey: (*She taps her baton.*) Hold it! Stop! Stop! Whatever is that noise?

Fidelia: It's me, Miss Toomey!

Alberto: Fidelia, oh no!

Carmela: Not here!

Miss Toomey: Fidelia, I should have known. Come over here, please.

(Fidelia, *with her homemade violin, goes to* Miss Toomey. Mrs. Reed *takes the violin from* Fidelia.)

Mrs. Reed: What is this, young lady?

Fidelia: It's a violin. I made it with some help from my brother and sister.

Mrs. Reed: It's very nice, Fidelia, but it doesn't belong in an orchestra. You can't play a tune on it.

Fidelia: Oh, but I *can* play a tune, Mrs. Reed. Listen! (*She begins to play ''The Man on the Flying Trapeze.''*) Buzz-zang-zang-zoong-zing! Buzz-zang-zang-zoong-zing . . .

(*Although the violin sounds strange, the melody of the song can be heard. When she finishes, everyone claps.*)

Mrs. Reed: That was very good, Fidelia! Where did you learn the correct hand positions for playing the violin?

Fidelia: I watched the other violin players. I did what Miss Toomey told them to do.

Mrs. Reed: How would you like to play a *real* violin, Fidelia?

Fidelia: I would love to, Mrs. Reed. But I'm too little, and not old enough yet.

Mrs. Reed: Oh, I don't know about that. (*to* Alberto) Are you Fidelia's brother?

Alberto: Yes.

Mrs. Reed: Well, I'd like you to do me a favor. My van is out in the parking lot. I'd like you to go there and . . . (*She whispers something in Alberto's ear.*)

Alberto: I'll be right back! (*He runs from the room, smiling.*)

Fidelia: Where is he going, Mrs. Reed?

Mrs. Reed: Just wait! You'll see.

Miss Toomey: (*to the audience*) None of us knew what Mrs. Reed was up to. Soon, however, Alberto returned, carrying the smallest violin case we had ever seen.

Alberto: Here it is.

Miss Toomey: (*to the audience*) Mrs. Reed opened the tiny case, and took out a beautiful little violin!

Mrs. Reed: This is a quarter-size violin, boys and girls. It is smaller than most violins. Let's see how it fits Fidelia.

Fidelia: (*She takes the violin and places it under her chin.*) It's perfect! My arms aren't too short, and it fits my fingers just fine!

Mrs. Reed: Fidelia, the boy who was using this violin has grown, so now he plays a bigger violin.

Fidelia: (*excited*) So you mean . . .

Mrs. Reed: That's right. How would you like to hold onto this one for awhile? Miss Toomey, do you think you can begin giving Fidelia violin lessons?

Miss Toomey: It would be my pleasure!

Fidelia: Does that mean I can play in the All City Orchestra?

Mrs. Reed: (*laughing*) No, not yet. But if you do as well as I think you will, I'm sure you will be in it next year.

Fidelia: Oh, boy!

Miss Toomey: (*to the audience*) But Alberto and Carmela *were* picked for the All City Orchestra that year. Fidelia and her father were proud of Alberto and Carmela as they performed in the concert. Fidelia didn't care if she wasn't in it this year. She had a violin exactly her own size, and her violin lessons had begun. As she clapped for her brother and sister, she knew that her day would come, too!

THE END

Reader's Response ❧ Some people may think that Fidelia was a pest. What did you think of her? Why?

Musical Instruments
Around the World

Banjo: U.S.A.

Bagpipes: Scotland

Koto: Japan

Steel drums: West Indies

Drums: Africa

Sitar: India

People all over the world play musical instruments. Some are similar and some are different. Look at this map and see where people play these special instruments. Which one would you like to play?

Ludwig van Beethoven:

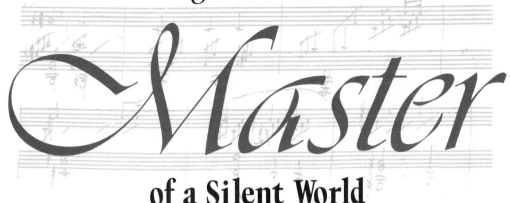

Master

of a Silent World

by Jeanette Leardi

In 1819, in the city of Vienna, Austria, Anton Schindler visited his friend Ludwig van Beethoven. When Anton arrived, Ludwig was playing the piano. The melody he played was beautiful, but there was something strange about the way he played the piano. As he played, he stamped his feet, and he sang out in a loud voice.

What was going on? Why did Ludwig stamp his feet and sing so loudly? Anton knew. His friend, the famous musician Ludwig van Beethoven, was writing a new piece of music. However, since Beethoven was completely deaf, he could not hear the loud sounds he made as he tried to imagine the sound of his music.

Beethoven's Early Life

How could this extraordinary man create music that he was unable to hear? Beethoven was not born deaf. He grew up hearing music practically all the time. He was born into a talented, musical family. His father, Johann van Beethoven, was a famous singer and a musician. He played the violin and clavier, an early form of piano. He was also a talented music instructor.

Beethoven learned to play music when he was a very young boy. He was only four years old when his father began giving him piano lessons. Soon after, he also learned to play the organ and violin. When he was only eight years old, he gave his first public concert, and by the time Beethoven was twelve, he was conducting an orchestra.

Beethoven loved to play music, but playing did not come easily to him. He had to practice for many hours. His hands were short, and sometimes he could not stretch his fingers to reach the notes that he wanted to play. Sometimes, when he found it difficult to play a piece of music, he would change the melody or make up a new melody. This surprised his teachers, but they knew that Beethoven had to be very talented to be able to do those things.

As Beethoven grew older, his father earned less and less money. Then, in 1787, his mother died. So Beethoven had to work hard to help support his father and his two younger brothers, Johann and Karl. To do this, Beethoven played in many, many piano concerts. Before long, his talent had made him famous.

Beethoven worked hard when he was composing new music.

Beethoven Creates Beautiful Music

In addition to playing music, Beethoven enjoyed creating new music. However, creating music was also difficult for him to do. It took him a long time to write a piece of music. Some of his greatest symphonies took him years to complete.

Why did it take Beethoven so long to write music? One reason was that he was very demanding of himself. He wanted each note to sound wonderful and important.

He usually started by writing bits and pieces of music. Then he would think about these short melodies and sometimes change them. Often he would cross out what he wrote and start all over again. A page of Beethoven's music looked messy and careless as he was writing it, but when it was finished and the music was performed, the sound that people heard was powerful and beautiful. They loved his music.

Beethoven Becomes Deaf

Music was the most important thing in Beethoven's life. Then, at the age of twenty-eight, he began to lose his hearing. At first, he heard a humming noise in his ears. Soon, he couldn't hear people when they talked softly to him. At the time, Beethoven thought that his problem was temporary and curable. But by 1801, the buzzing noise grew worse. It bothered him day and night. He tried everything he could think of to find a cure. He sought out doctors, and took special baths and medicines, but nothing worked.

Beethoven didn't want his friends to know that he was becoming deaf, so he stayed away from them. He no longer went to parties. He even took long walks in the countryside to escape the city noises that hurt his ears.

By 1802, Beethoven was so unhappy and angry that he almost decided to give up writing and performing music. In a letter to his brothers he wrote, "How terrible I feel that someone who stands beside me can hear a flute in the distance, or a shepherd singing, and I cannot." Beethoven did not know what to do.

Beethoven used an ear trumpet to improve his hearing.

Yet Beethoven knew in his heart that he was meant to write great music. So he decided that he would continue to write and perform. He also made up his mind to live differently. He began using a special object called an ear trumpet to hear what few sounds he could. He also carried a notebook or a chalkboard on which people wrote the things they wanted to say to him. He did eventually give up playing piano concerts, but he composed more music than he ever had before.

These are Beethoven's instruments.

Beethoven Composes His Greatest Music

In the years after 1802, Beethoven composed his greatest music. His love of music and his talent were so great that he didn't need his ears to hear the music he wrote. He listened instead with his mind and his heart.

By 1819, Beethoven was totally deaf, but his music was even more powerful than before. In 1824, Beethoven conducted an orchestra that was playing his Ninth Symphony for the first time. The symphony ended with a song of joy. When it was over, the audience stood up and clapped and cheered. However, Beethoven was not facing the audience, so he did not know how much they had enjoyed his music. Then one of the musicians on stage turned the great man around so he could see the audience. Beethoven saw the audience smiling and cheering wildly. Even though he could not hear his music, he could tell by the audience's reaction that it was very, very special. Without a doubt, Beethoven had learned to master his silent world.

Reader's Response ∽ What do you admire most about Beethoven? Why?

THE

Toy Symphony

MUSIC OR GAME?

Did you know that a toy symphony is a real musical work? It is called a toy symphony because some members of the orchestra use toys to play the music.

A famous Toy Symphony was written in the late 1700s. The music calls for these toy instruments: trumpet, drum, rattle, triangle, and three instruments that imitated bird sounds—a cuckoo, a quail, and a nightingale. Because none of these toys can actually play a tune, the symphony also includes real violins and a double bass.

Nobody knows for sure who wrote the symphony. We may never know the truth.

Later, other composers wrote toy symphonies. Have you ever heard one?

Beethoven's Biggest Fan

Charles Schulz has entertained people with his *Peanuts* comic strip for a long time. We see Charlie Brown, Snoopy, Lucy, Schroeder, and the rest of the *Peanuts* gang in newspapers, books, on television, and at the movies.

Each of the *Peanuts* characters is special in some way. Snoopy would like to fly planes. Lucy likes to tell the others what to do. Charlie Brown wants everyone to like him. And Schroeder wishes he could play the piano like Ludwig van Beethoven. In fact, Schroeder is Beethoven's biggest fan. How can you tell? Read the comic strips on these pages for clues.

by Charles M. Schulz

From "Peanuts" by Charles Schulz. Reprinted by permission of United Feature Syndicate, Inc.

From "Peanuts" by Charles Schulz. Reprinted by permission of United Feature Syndicate, Inc.

Doctor De Soto

written and illustrated by William Steig

Doctor De Soto, the dentist, did very good work, so he had no end of patients. Those close to his own size—moles, chipmunks, et cetera—sat in the regular dentist's chair.

Larger animals sat on the floor, while Doctor De Soto stood on a ladder.

For extra-large animals, he had a special room. There Doctor De Soto was hoisted up to the patient's mouth by his assistant, who also happened to be his wife.

Doctor De Soto was especially popular with the big animals. He was able to work inside their mouths, wearing rubbers to keep his feet dry; and his fingers were so delicate, and his drill so dainty, they could hardly feel any pain.

Being a mouse, he refused to treat animals dangerous to mice, and it said so on his sign. When the doorbell rang, he and his wife would look out the window. They wouldn't admit even the most timid-looking cat.

One day, when they looked out, they saw a well-dressed fox with a flannel bandage around his jaw.

"I cannot treat you, sir!" Doctor De Soto shouted. "Sir! Haven't you read my sign?"

"Please!" the fox wailed. "Have mercy, I'm suffering!" And he wept so bitterly it was pitiful to see.

"Just a moment," said Doctor De Soto. "That poor fox," he whispered to his wife. "What shall we do?"

"Let's risk it," said Mrs. De Soto. She pressed the buzzer and let the fox in.

209

He was up the stairs in a flash. "Bless your little hearts," he cried, falling to his knees. "I beg you, *do* something! My tooth is killing me."

"Sit on the floor, sir," said Doctor De Soto, "and remove the bandage, please."

Doctor De Soto climbed up the ladder and bravely entered the fox's mouth. "Ooo-wow!" he gasped. The fox had a rotten bicuspid and unusually bad breath.

"This tooth will have to come out," Doctor De Soto announced. "But we can make you a new one."

"Just stop the pain," whimpered the fox, wiping some tears away.

Despite his misery, he realized he had a tasty little morsel in his mouth, and his jaw began to quiver. "Keep open!" yelled Doctor De Soto. "Wide open!" yelled his wife.

"I'm giving you gas now," said Doctor De Soto. "You won't feel a thing when I yank that tooth."

Soon the fox was in dreamland. "M-m-m, yummy," he mumbled. "How I love them raw . . . with just a pinch of salt and a . . . dry . . . white wine."

They could guess what he was dreaming about. Mrs. De Soto handed her husband a pole to keep the fox's mouth open.

Doctor De Soto fastened his extractor to the bad tooth. Then he and his wife began turning the winch. Finally, with a sucking sound, the tooth popped out and hung swaying in the air.

"I'm bleeding!" the fox yelped when he came to.

Doctor De Soto ran up the ladder and stuffed some gauze in the hole. "The worst is over," he said. "I'll have your new tooth ready tomorrow. Be here at eleven sharp."

The fox, still woozy, said goodbye and left. On his way home, he wondered if it would be shabby of him to eat the De Sotos when the job was done.

After office hours, Mrs. De Soto molded a tooth of pure gold and polished it. "Raw with salt, indeed," muttered Doctor De Soto. "How foolish to trust a fox!"

"He didn't know what he was saying," said Mrs. De Soto. "Why should he harm us? We're helping him."

"Because he's a fox!" said Doctor De Soto. "They're wicked, wicked creatures."

That night the De Sotos lay awake worrying. "Should we let him in tomorrow?" Mrs. De Soto wondered.

"Once I start a job," said the dentist firmly, "I finish it. My father was the same way."

"But we must do something to protect ourselves," said his wife. They talked and talked until they formed a plan. "I think it will work," said Doctor De Soto. A minute later he was snoring.

The next morning, promptly at eleven, a very cheerful fox turned up. He was feeling not a particle of pain.

When Doctor De Soto got into his mouth, he snapped it shut for a moment, then opened wide and laughed. "Just a joke!" he chortled.

"Be serious," said the dentist sharply. "We have work to do." His wife was lugging the heavy tooth up the ladder.

"Oh, I love it!" exclaimed the fox. "It's just beautiful."

Doctor De Soto set the gold tooth in its socket and hooked it up to the teeth on both sides.

The fox caressed the new tooth with his tongue. "My, it feels good," he thought. "I really shouldn't eat them. On the other hand, how can I resist?"

"We're not finished," said Doctor De Soto, holding up a large jug. "I have here a remarkable preparation developed only recently by my wife and me. With just one application, you can be rid of toothaches forever. How would you like to be the first one to receive this unique treatment?"

"I certainly would!" the fox declared. "I'd be honored." He hated any kind of personal pain.

"You will never have to see us again," said Doctor De Soto.

"*No one* will see you again," said the fox to himself. He had definitely made up his mind to eat them—with the help of his brand-new tooth.

Doctor De Soto stepped into the fox's mouth with a bucket of secret formula and proceeded to paint each tooth. He hummed as he worked. Mrs. De Soto stood by on the ladder, pointing out spots he had missed. The fox looked very happy.

When the dentist was done, he stepped out. "Now close your jaws tight," he said, "and keep them closed for a full minute." The fox did as he was told. Then he tried to open his mouth—but his teeth were stuck together!

"Ah, excuse me, I should have mentioned," said Doctor De Soto, "you won't be able to open your mouth for a day or two. The secret formula must first permeate the dentine. But don't worry. No pain ever again!"

The fox was stunned. He stared at Doctor De Soto, then at his wife. They smiled, and waited. All he could do was say, "Frank oo berry mush" through his clenched teeth, and get up and leave. He tried to do so with dignity.

Then he stumbled down the stairs in a daze.

Doctor De Soto and his assistant had outfoxed the fox. They kissed each other and took the rest of the day off.

Reader's Response ∼ What made this story funny to you?

Library Link ∼ *William Steig has written and illustrated other books you might enjoy reading. One of them is* Yellow and Pink.

Did You Know...

Some animals grow only one set of teeth. Some grow two sets. Some have no teeth at all. And a few, like some reptiles, grow a new tooth as often as one is lost.

A giraffe has no upper front teeth. There is a hard thick pad where teeth would ordinarily be.

The elephant's tusks are the largest teeth in the world. One pair of tusks at a zoo in New York weighs 293 pounds. Each tusk is more than eleven feet long.

A tiger shark has more than one row of teeth, with new rows forming all the time behind the front row. When a tooth is lost, the tooth behind it moves forward and replaces it.

Can you name some animals that have no teeth?

(Answer: turtles, birds, some insects)

Why do you suppose this is so?

215

AMY'S GOOSE

written by Efner Tudor Holmes

illustrated by Tasha Tudor

Amy stood in the garden watching the sun sink behind the hills. She had been helping her parents dig the last of the potatoes. The air smelled of cool, damp earth mixed with the scent of the gold and orange leaves that fell silently and incessantly to the ground.

Then Amy heard the cry she had been waiting for all fall. Her face turned eagerly to the sky, and she saw the long V of the wild geese. Their call was faint at first, then louder as they flew closer. The cry fell down to her, carrying with it the spirit of all wild things. The geese began to break their formation as they came near the lake at the edge of the potato field. Amy knew that they would settle there for the night.

They always did and she had a large sack of corn in the barn, all ready for them. Usually a flock would settle at night and by daybreak be off again on its long journey south. Many times, in other years, Amy had seen the geese rise up through the morning mist. They would circle aimlessly for a moment and then the great long V would take shape and Amy would watch them as they flew away. In her mind, she could still hear their cry. To her, they seemed to be calling good-bye and she would be filled with loneliness. For Amy was an only child and the wild creatures were her friends.

But now the geese were over her, and coming in low. They were so close that Amy could feel the wind from their great white wings. She stood, a small, still figure, as the geese flew past her and landed in the lake and on its shores.

Someone called to her and she turned to see her father walking down the garden. He stood beside her and put an arm around her shoulders.

"Well, little one," he said. "I see your friends have come back. As soon as we get these potatoes under cover and eat dinner, we'll get that sack of corn."

"Aren't they beautiful?" Amy asked him. "And there are a lot more of them this year."

Her father grinned down at her.

"That's because they've been spreading the word about a lake where a little girl will be waiting with a hundred pounds of good corn," he teased her. "Now come, it's almost dark and we've got to get these potatoes in."

Dinner seemed to Amy to be taking unusually long. Ordinarily she loved sitting there in the dining room with all three of them together, and the candles casting soft shadows on the warm wood-paneled walls. The room smelled of freshly baked apple and pumpkin pies. But Amy's thoughts were with the geese out on the moonlit lake. *Her* geese, she thought. They had remembered, and had come back to her again! She could hardly wait to go out to them, and to bring them some corn. It was a ritual she had kept up since one fall when the snow came early and some geese had stayed longer than usual. Amy had felt sorry for them and worried that they wouldn't have enough to eat. So she had scattered corn for them.

At last her father pushed back his chair and stood up. Amy got her sweater and followed him out to the barn. He hoisted the sack of corn to his shoulder and together Amy and her father walked down through the garden and into the field by the lake. The stillness of the night was broken only by the crickets singing their lonely song of the end of summer.

All at once they heard the frantic honking of a goose. Then the flock began to pick up its cry and Amy could hear their wings beating on the water. As she ran down the field she saw many geese rising up into the air in confusion and fright. Others stayed on the shore, standing with their long necks stretched low to the ground as they gabbled in alarm.

"It's a fox," her father cried. "Look, he's got
one." Dropping the sack of corn he picked up a rock
and flung it at the fox. Amy ran at him clapping her
hands and yelling. The fox let go of the goose and fled.
But the goose lay still. On its white neck Amy saw a
spreading spot of blood. She kneeled down and, as
gently as she could, she picked up the big bird. The
frightened goose beat its wings and tried to fly away but
it was too feeble to struggle for long. Soon it lay
quietly, its wings drooped over Amy's legs and onto the
sand. Amy's father squatted down to look.

"It may not really be as bad as it looks," he said.
"I think we can save her. Let's get her up to the barn."

He lifted the goose from Amy's arms and they
headed back up the field. Amy turned once to look
toward the lake. All was quiet again and Amy saw
several geese nibbling at the sack of corn they had
forgotten on the shore.

When Amy went to look at the wounded goose the
next morning, she was surprised to see it standing up
and pecking at a dish of feed. But it was obviously still
in some pain. Amy went slowly into the pen. She held
out her hand but the goose hissed at her fiercely and
retreated to a far corner. So the goose and the girl sat
for several minutes regarding each other.

"It's all right," Amy said softly. "You're safe here."

Amy spent most of the rest of the day with the
goose. That evening the wild creature ate a few grains
of corn from her hand. And when she stroked its head,
the goose would gabble in what Amy felt sure was
affection. A very special feeling for the big white bird
was growing in her. She wondered hopefully if she'd be
able to tame it. Amy thought it would be a real gift to
have this wild bird place its trust in her.

For several days Amy was so busy taking care of
her goose that she didn't stop to think it strange that the
other geese had not left the lake to continue their
journey to the warm South. One late afternoon, Amy
and the white goose were out on the lawn. Amy was
eating an apple and giving bits of it to the goose.

Suddenly they heard the cry of a goose overhead. Amy looked up to see a lone bird flying over the barn. It would circle silently, then start up its cry.

Amy's goose stood listening intently, with her head cocked to one side, looking up into the sky at the other bird. Then she began answering his call and flapping her wings. She ran over to Amy and nibbled at a piece of apple, but then she stood listening again. On the lake, Amy saw the rest of the flock. They had not left! They were waiting for her goose . . . and that must be her mate calling to her!

"Come on," she said to the goose, "I'm going to shut you up. You're not strong enough for flying yet. Next spring they'll be back."

Amy put the goose in its pen in the barn, closed the door firmly, and went to help her mother fix dinner. But all evening she felt upset. The warm house seemed to hold her in, like a cage. She thought of her goose, of the wild creature she had shut in the barn. She knew that the goose *was* really well enough for the long flight now. And she thought of the white gander flying alone over the barn calling to his mate.

She slipped out of the house and went through the shadow-filled garden and down to the lake. It was a cold night and mist was drifting up from the lake into the moonlight. Amy felt an eerie restlessness. Then she saw the geese. They, too, were restless. Several of them would rise up and call to the others, then drop back into the water. Others stood clustered on the shore as if holding a meeting.

Suddenly, they all rose up into the sky together. Their farewell cry filled the air and Amy watched them fall into flight formation. She would see no more geese until spring. Winter was coming. Amy knew it and obviously the geese sensed it, too. The flock had already grown small in the distant sky when Amy saw a lone bird drop out and begin flying back. Amy knew where it was headed.

She began running up the field. As she came to the barn, she heard the cry of the lone gander in the cold air and then the muffled honking that answered him from the barn. She flung open the door and ran to the pen where she had put her goose. The white goose was frantically pushing against the wire. When she saw Amy she stretched out her long neck and gabbled. Amy kneeled down. She put her arms around the big bird, and the goose put her beak in the curve of Amy's neck. Amy began to cry. She held the bird tightly, wishing it could stay. Then she picked up the white bird and carried her out into the night.

They stood silently together for a moment, until the goose set up a cry and began to run and beat her wings. Amy could hear the gander answering and as she watched, the goose rose into the moonlight. Her mate joined her and together they flew, following the flock before them.

Amy stood alone in the night and wiped away her tears. She felt the cold ground under her bare feet and thought of Spring, when she would be standing by the lake watching a flock of white geese fly over her and into the water.

Reader's Response ～ Do you think Amy made the right choice? Would you have done the same thing?

Library Link ～ *If you liked* Amy's Goose, *you may want to read* Carrie's Gift, *another book written by Efner Tudor Holmes.*

Weather or Not

Come rain, come snow,
come heat, come hail...

Why is everybody
interested in the
weather?

UMBRELLAS IN THE RAIN, *painting by Maurice Prendergast, 1899, American, 1859-1924, Watercolor, 14" x 20 7/8" (355 x 530 mm), Charles Henry Hayden Fund, Museum of Fine Arts, Boston*

Theme Books for
Weather or Not

What's your favorite kind of weather? No matter what kind of weather is heading your way, come to where the seasons change and where weather can be a fearsome thing!

When Anna and Grandpa set out one snowy morning, they think they are going to school. But when they are stranded by a blizzard in *Anna, Grandpa, and the Big Storm* by Carla Stevens, how will they get home?

✥ What is it like to live where there is always snow and ice? Polar bears know. Explore the Arctic with a polar bear mother and her two cubs in **Polar Bear Cubs** by Downs Matthews. Find out how they survive in this frozen, dangerous land.

More Books to Enjoy

The Terrible Eek by Patricia A. Compton
Stopping by Woods on a Snowy Evening
    by Robert Frost
Cloudy with a Chance of Meatballs
    by Judi Barrett
First Snow by Helen Coutant

The Wind and the Sun

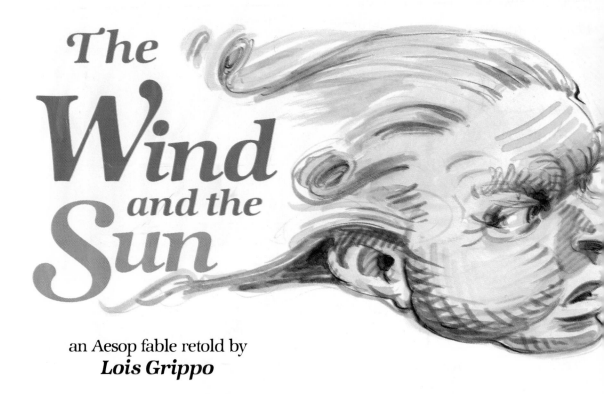

an Aesop fable retold by
Lois Grippo

Sun was smiling to herself in the morning sky. She had just woken up and was about to share her bright smile with the earth. Suddenly, there was a great whoosh of air. The whoosh was so strong that it blew a cloud right across Sun's morning face.

"Good morning, Sunshine," a voice boomed out. It was Wind. "How are you today, my little friend?" she whooshed. "As a matter of fact, where are you?" Wind said. "You seem to be covered by a cloud." Then Wind threw back her curly head and laughed. She laughed so hard, the cloud in front of Sun's face blew right away.

Sun smiled kindly into Wind's face. "Good morning, Wind," she said. "Are you all right? You seem all out of breath! Did you use too much of your strength blowing that cloud in front of my face?"

"If you think that took strength, you are not as bright as you think," Wind puffed. "All I did was yawn."

Sun smiled so sweetly that all the flowers on the earth popped out of the ground and looked up at her. "Oh, my," she said. "Sometimes I forget my own strength. It is much too early for the flowers to bloom."

"You call that strength!" Wind shouted. Then she breathed in very deeply and let out a powerful gust of air. The poor flowers shook. Their petals blew off and whirled in the air. Even the trees shook and bent. "Now that's strength," Wind boasted. "And I hardly even tried."

"Oh, Wind," Sun said. "Don't be so puffed-up all the time. You are strong, that's true. But, I am stronger."

"Come on, Sun," Wind said. "Don't get so hot under the collar. You are strong, I suppose. But, *I* am stronger!"

Now, Wind and Sun had argued many times about who was stronger. Wind would huff, and Sun would sweetly shine. Wind would puff, and Sun would sweetly shine. It seemed like an argument that had no winner. Then one day, Sun had an idea.

"Let's have a contest," Sun said to her windy friend.

"It will be no contest at all," Wind boasted. "I will win, of course. You will learn once and for all that I am the stronger!"

Sun just smiled calmly. She filled the sky with her warm rays.

"What will the contest be?" Wind asked.

Sun looked down and saw a man with a long beard walking down the road. He was wearing a heavy cape around his shoulders. "See that man," Sun said to Wind. "The contest will be to see who can make him take off his cape."

"Good!" said Wind. "That should take me just a second or two. I am in a hurry, you know. I have to start a hurricane this afternoon."

"Since you are in such a rush," Sun said, "why don't you go first?"

"That's fine with me," Wind said. "Watch this!"

Wind caught some air in her cheeks and began to puff up. She blew up like a balloon. Then, Wind opened her mouth and out rushed a gust of air. When the air reached the earth, the man's hair began to blow a bit, but he didn't even notice.

"I was just warming up a bit," Wind said. "Now, I'll really get to work."

With that, Wind blew even harder. Everything shook. Windows rattled. Tree branches snapped. The air was full of flying objects. The man's hair and beard blew this way and that. His hands grew cold, and his face burned from the wind. But the man did not lose his cape. He held it tightly around him. The harder Wind blew, the colder the man became and the tighter he clung to his cape.

"Would you like to rest awhile and catch your breath?" Sun asked.

"Don't get so overheated," Wind growled. "I was just trying to make the contest exciting. Now, I'll show you what I can really do."

Wind took a deep, deep breath. She drew in great mouthfuls of air until she was bigger than the world's largest blimp! Then, she opened her mouth. There was a tremendous roar as all the air rushed out.

Dark storm clouds filled the sky. The whirling, swirling air hit the earth. It blew so hard that the water in the lakes turned into great waves. Huge oak trees were bent in half. Birds that were flying south were pushed backward toward the north. Still the shivering man did not lose his cape! The fierce winds just made him hold on to it even more tightly.

At last, Wind was tired out. She was too tired to blow even the tiniest breeze. Everything on the earth stood still. The storm clouds slowly drifted away. It was Sun's turn.

Sun calmly turned her face toward the earth. She gently shone down on its green fields. She gently shone on the man walking down the road. The man raised one hand to cover his eyes. With the other hand, he still held on to his cape.

"See! See!" said Wind. "You are no stronger than I am." Wind was still very tired. Those few words took all the breath she could manage.

Sun smiled calmly at her worn-out friend. "Just rest," she said. "I will try again."

Sun turned back to the earth. She shone more brightly. The air grew warmer and warmer. Soon the man began to feel more comfortable. He undid the buttons on his cape, though he still held on to it with one hand. Sun was not upset, but Wind was starting to get back some of her strength.

"Face it!" Wind breezed. "If I could not loosen his cape, surely you cannot."

Sun did not lose her temper. She just continued to smile warmly down on the man. The warmth of her rays caused the man to become very hot. The man smiled in Sun's pleasant warmth. Soon he was too hot to keep his cape on. The man gladly removed it from his shoulders.

"See!" said Sun. "Now tell me which of us is the stronger!"

Wind looked as though all of the air had gone out of her. For once, she had absolutely nothing to say. Wind knew all too well who had won the contest. Sun was the stronger!

LESSON: *You can do more with gentleness than you can do with force.*

Reader's Response ～ Think of a time when you used gentleness instead of force. Did it work better?

Library Link ～ *Aesop lived in Greece more than 2500 years ago. If you would like to read other fables by Aesop, try* The Fox and the Crow *and* The Lion and the Mouse.

A Powerful FUTURE

At this solar power plant, which operated in California during the 1980s, groups of mirrors collected solar energy and reflected it onto solar energy collectors.

When it comes to making electricity, wind and sun are both winners! They are clean, plentiful, and, yes, powerful.

Some modern solar power plants use mirrors to collect the sun's energy, which is then made into electricity. Some scientists predict that one day the sun will replace oil as a major source of power.

For years people have used windmills to pump water and grind grain. Today, windmills used to make electricity are often called wind turbines. Some have specially-designed blades that look like airplane propellers.

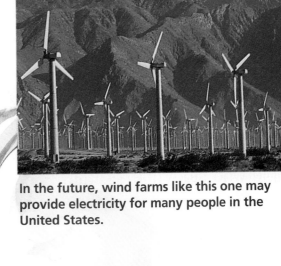

In the future, wind farms like this one may provide electricity for many people in the United States.

AN INTERVIEW WITH A

Meteorologist

BY GEORGE PORTER

George is fascinated by the way weather changes. He wants to know about weather and how meteorologists, people who study the air that surrounds the earth, forecast changes in the weather. A friend of his parents, Antonio Alfonso Dreumont, is a meteorologist. For a science project at school, George wrote to Mr. Dreumont to ask if he could interview him. Mr. Dreumont agreed.

GEORGE: Where did you grow up?

MR. DREUMONT: I grew up in Brownsville, a city on the southern coast of Texas.

GEORGE: Did the weather there make you curious about how and why weather changes?

MR. DREUMONT: Yes! The weather in South Texas often changes very quickly. A day can start out warm with clear skies, and by the afternoon there is thunder, lightning, and pouring rain. These sudden changes fascinated me, and made me very curious about the reasons for changes in the weather.

GEORGE: How long have you been a meteorologist?

MR. DREUMONT: I have been a meteorologist for 24 years.

GEORGE: When did you first decide to become a meteorologist?

MR. DREUMONT: The idea first came to me when I was in high school. I had to write a term paper on hurricanes. It was the first time that I did research on weather. I used books and magazines, reading everything I could find about hurricanes. The more I read, the more I wanted to read. I knew then that when I went to college, I would study meteorology. After college, I became an assistant at the Brownsville Weather Bureau.

GEORGE: What did you learn at the Brownsville Weather Bureau?

MR. DREUMONT: It was there that I really learned how to be a meteorologist. I learned how to tell airplane pilots about weather conditions. It was my job to give pilots a description of the kinds of weather they were flying into. I also learned how to make farming forecasts. These forecasts warned farmers if the land was too cold to start planting, or when it was wet and warm and therefore a good time to plant. Perhaps the most important thing I learned was how to read radar. Radar makes it possible to see conditions that affect the weather, beyond what you can see with your eyes.

wind speed 80 mph

Tornadoes can cause a lot of damage.

GEORGE: Where else have you worked?

MR. DREUMONT: I have worked in many different places. I worked in Georgia, where I saw thunderstorms and tornadoes. I worked in San Francisco, California, where the weather is ideal. It never gets too hot or too cold, and most of the time the sun is shining. I worked in Washington, D.C., at the National Headquarters of the Weather Service. Then, in 1981, I moved to Boise, Idaho. There I began to specialize in forecasting forest fires.

GEORGE: How do you forecast forest fires?

MR. DREUMONT: Idaho is in the northwestern part of our country. The weather here is sometimes very dry. If we have a mild winter, there is little snow to melt in the spring. Therefore, the trees and grasses tend to be very dry. This becomes a problem when we get dry thunderstorms. During a dry thunderstorm, rain evaporates before it hits the ground and lightning bolts strike. When that happens, the chance of forest fires increases. When I see those conditions, I warn people about the danger of possible forest fires.

GEORGE: Have you shared your experience forecasting forest fires with other meteorologists?

MR. DREUMONT: Yes! Because I speak Spanish, I have had the opportunity to teach courses on the detection and prevention of forest fires in Ecuador, Chile, Argentina, Venezuela, and Spain. Working in all of those countries has made it possible for me to meet and talk with many other meteorologists. Together, we talk about the problems we share in forecasting weather, and the use of new technology to help solve those problems. These experiences have helped me to become a better meteorologist.

GEORGE: What do you do on a typical day at the National Weather Service in Boise?

MR. DREUMONT: The first thing I do is use the computer to check weather forecasts and to look at weather maps of the atmosphere. The atmosphere, or the air that surrounds the earth, is described in numerical units on the computer. These units tell about the conditions in the atmosphere. I use that information to lead a staff discussion on weather conditions. We talk about whether the rivers are high and could cause flooding. We decide if wind conditions may cause problems for airplane pilots. If it's the fire season, we talk about the kind of weather conditions that increase the chance of fires. Then we send up a weather balloon that carries an instrument called a radiosonde. The radiosonde measures temperatures, wind, humidity, or moisture in the air, and atmospheric pressure in the upper atmosphere. Then we use the information gathered by the radiosonde to forecast the weather.

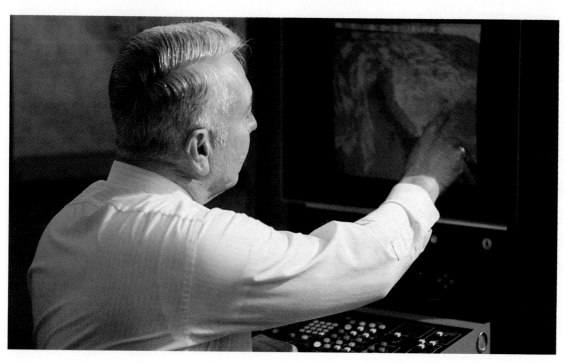

Mr. Dreumont checks a map on his computer screen.

Mr. Dreumont releases a weather balloon.

GEORGE: What other instruments do you use and what information do you get from them?

MR. DREUMONT: We use a ceilometer to tell us the height of the clouds from the ground. This information is important for pilots. If the clouds are too close to the ground, pilots might have trouble seeing the runway as they prepare to land. To check the temperature, we use wet and dry bulb thermometers. The anemometer measures wind speed, and the weather vane shows the wind's direction. Humidity is measured by a hygrometer. And we use computers to find out the relative humidity, or the amount of moisture in the air in relation to the temperature.

GEORGE: Do you use computers to forecast the weather?

MR. DREUMONT: Yes, we do. Computers are one of the most important tools meteorologists have. Computers can give us a reasonable guess as to what tomorrow's weather will be. But it is up to the meteorologist to check the accuracy of the computer. He or she does that by looking at the numerical units that the computer uses to describe the atmosphere, and then evaluating those units based on additional information that is supplied by weather instruments. Together, this information makes it possible for a meteorologist to forecast the weather.

GEORGE: How does weather forecasting help people?

MR. DREUMONT: People in many industries make

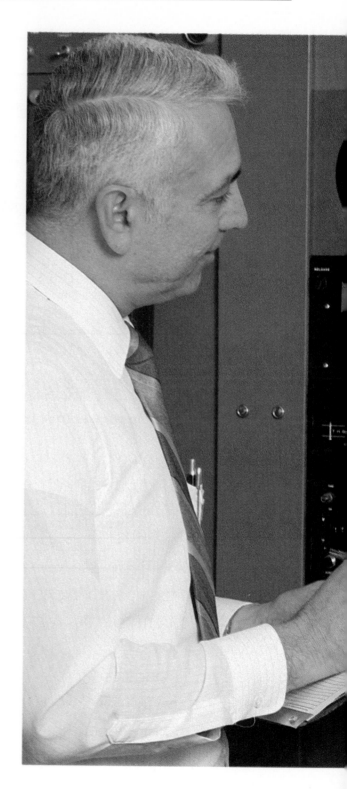

decisions based on weather conditions. Farmers need to know when a cold front is coming so they can protect their crops. Airlines need to know if stormy weather will delay flights. Construction workers cannot build homes if the weather is too cold or too wet. You and I need to know if there is an emergency, such as a hurricane or a flood.

GEORGE: What are the hardest things to forecast?

MR. DREUMONT: Big events, such as floods, droughts, and blizzards, are difficult to forecast. Deciding when rain will turn to snow is difficult. It can also be hard to forecast when the temperature will drop to its lowest point during the night.

◄ **Instruments help meteorologists forecast the weather.**

Mr. Dreumont takes time to enjoy some sunny weather.

GEORGE: Why do you like being a meteorologist?

MR. DREUMONT: My job is fun all the time. No two days are ever alike. Weather is not only my job, it is my hobby. For 48 years of my life, meteorology has been my love. I love to watch a thunderstorm. I love to look out my window and watch the beauty of a snowstorm. The beauty of nature and the changes that weather brings make my job interesting to me.

Reader's Response ∾ What do you think is the most fascinating part of Mr. Dreumont's job? Why?

Stormy Weather

Lightning flashing across the sky is actually a flash of electricity. Electricity also produces the light in an electric light bulb, but a lightning flash is much more powerful.

The electric current heats the air. Thunder is the sound that is made as the heated air expands. You hear thunder after you see lightning because sound travels more slowly than light. You can tell how far away lightning is by counting the number of seconds between the flash and the thunder. The sound of thunder takes about five seconds to travel one mile.

Lightning can be dangerous to people and nature. The safest place during a thunderstorm is indoors.

Lightning can also start fires. Many forest fires begin this way. In 1988, forest fires swept through Yellowstone National Park. Lightning started most of the fires, damaging trees and meadows in more than a third of the park.

Mississippi Possum

by Miska Miles

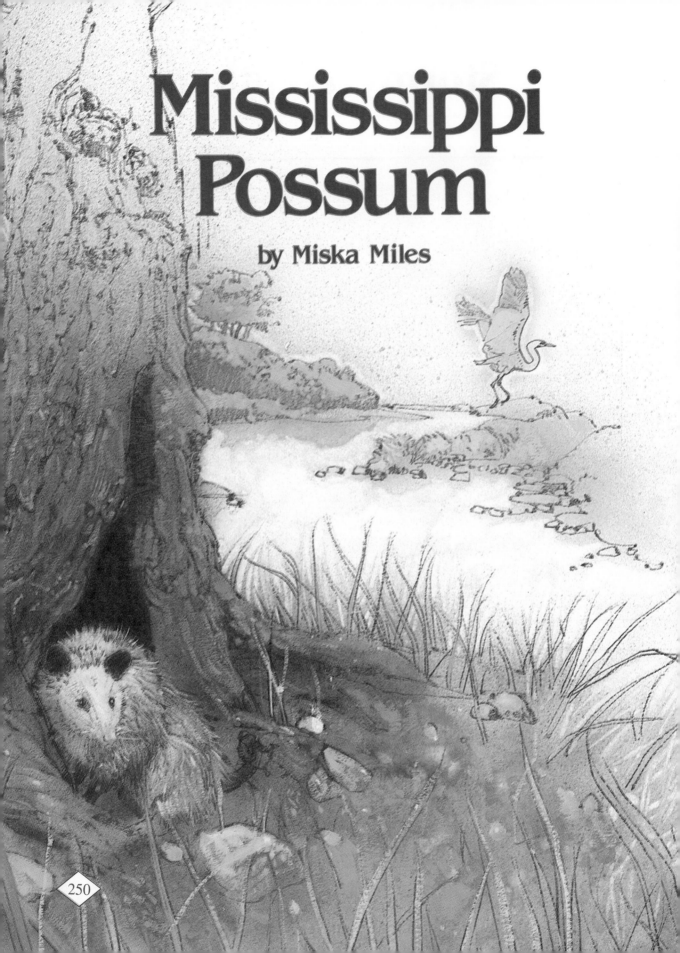

Near the Mississippi River, a little gray possum lived in a hollow log.

When he was afraid, which was much of the time, he crept into the log and waited there.

He was afraid of many things. He was afraid of hawks and owls, of bobcats and foxes. And he was afraid of people.

When people came near, he ran into the log and was as still as he knew how to be.

There were things he was not afraid of. He was not afraid of mice or snakes, birds' eggs or berries. These, he ate.

Now, for a long time the rain had fallen and the river water rose and spread out farther along the banks. The possum looked around for food, for he had found nothing to eat for a day.

He looked up into a tree that grew beside the river, and he knew there was a bird's nest high in the branches.

He climbed up above the nest, and held a branch with his back foot, and swung by his tail to look into the nest. The nest was empty.

He climbed down again, and he looked around for berries. While he was looking he felt the earth tremble with footsteps, and he knew that something was coming down the hill, and he was afraid. He ran into his hollow log and was as still as a wild animal can be.

Jefferson Jackson and his sister Rose Mary came down the hill to look at the river.

"Look at that old Mississippi," Jefferson said. "It's getting higher and higher."

For a minute they watched. "It's coming this way," Rose Mary said. She pointed to a little stick lying on the ground. "Watch. The water's touching it." They waited.

"And now the stick's floating off," Jefferson said. "River's coming. Let's tell Papa."

They ran, pounding their feet hard against the ground.

When everything was quiet, the possum came out from his log. The brown river water was creeping along the ground toward him. Now a leaf held it back, then on it came, pushing its slow way—

He turned to go up the hill.

He traveled a long time and he came to a little brown house. He hurried past, for he knew that people lived there.

In this house, Jefferson and Rose Mary were talking to their mother and father.

"We could see the river coming higher while we watched," Jefferson said.

"Right up the hill," said Rose Mary.

"We know," said their mother. "We were about to look for you. We're going up to higher ground, where it's safe."

Quickly she reached for a basket and packed it with corn bread and a cherry pie and a handful of berries.

"The news came over the radio," their father said. "Everybody has to get out. The river's so high that it's breaking through the levee. If it breaks in many more places, it could flood right over this land. Hurry."

"Will we come back?" Rose Mary asked.

"We'll be back when the river goes down," her father said.

"That old river will pour a lot of water into the Gulf," Jefferson said. "Then everything will be just as it's always been."

Now, all this time the possum was trudging up the hill, and he saw many things.

He saw a rabbit and a dog traveling along together and the dog didn't chase the rabbit. He saw a fox and a wild turkey and the fox didn't kill the turkey.

And behind him he heard the river, and he knew he must run from it.

He heard something coming close behind him. Something else was running from the river.

There was no tree he could climb and the grasses were not thick enough for hiding. He lay down on the ground and he didn't move.

Rose Mary and Jefferson and their mother and father came up the hill.

"Look at the poor little old dead possum," Rose Mary said.

When everything was still, the possum slowly got to his feet and looked around. The river was crowding up the slope of the hill. A log floated past—maybe his own log. A boat went by and it was full of people. He saw a table floating on the water.

Far ahead were people on their way to the top of the hill, and some drove cows before them, and others led horses—

At the top of the hill, a soldier spoke to Mr. Jackson. "We have a tent for you," he said. "And there's plenty of hot food ready. Before long you'll be home again."

Rose Mary and Jefferson and their parents stood in line for food and for warm gray blankets. And afterward, they went into their tent and lay down on the earth to sleep.

"Wrapped in that blanket, you look like a gray log," Jefferson said.

But Rose Mary didn't hear, for she was asleep.

Night came, and the possum felt his way through the grasses with his whiskers. When he finally reached the top of the dark hill, he was hungry and tired. He looked in the first tent, and he thought he saw four gray logs lying on the ground.

He sniffed the nearest. He smelled an enemy.

Rose Mary sat up. "Papa," she said. "Papa. I heard something."

Her father snapped on a flashlight. "I don't see anything," he said.

"There's another little dead possum," she said.

"Maybe it's not dead," Jefferson said. "Maybe it's only pretending. They do, you know."

"He's an ugly fellow," her father said.

"I think he's nice-looking, for a possum," Rose Mary said. She sat down beside him and touched his rough fur. "He feels cold. He feels dead."

"Put something to eat in front of his nose and see what happens," Jefferson said.

"There are some berries in the basket," his mother said.

Rose Mary put the berries on the ground close to the possum's pointed nose.

The possum lay for a long time as though he were dead, and he hardly dared breathe, he was so frightened. Then he smelled something so good that he had to get up and look around.

The people didn't move and he was very hungry.

He ate the berries. They were fat and ripe and good. And when he had finished, the father reached out his hand, and the possum was afraid. He knew he had to climb high to be safe. He ran up along Rose Mary's arm, and she didn't move. He sat on her shoulder.

This was better than a tree. He was warm and comfortable. It was almost as good as a hollow log.

"He's getting tame," Rose Mary said. "When
we go home, we can take him with us."

And during the days that passed while they
waited to go home, planes flew overhead and
looked for people and animals who needed help.

Steamboats churned the yellow water and
pulled barges loaded with people and animals who
had been rescued from the roofs of houses and
barns.

Levees were built and made strong to hold
the great river. And as the time passed, the possum
grew tamer. He followed Rose Mary everywhere.

After a while, the river was caught behind the new levees, and it was time for everyone to go back home.

Jefferson and his mother and father and sister started down the hill, and the possum sat on Rose Mary's shoulder all the way to the little brown house near the bottom of the hill.

Then they were home, and there was a mark high on the wall to show that the Mississippi River had risen almost to the ceiling.

The possum found a hollow log near the back door to live in. Sometimes he came out and sat on Rose Mary's shoulder. More often he hunted for mushrooms or mice, and he wasn't afraid— much of the time.

Reader's Response ∿ Which part of this story seemed most real to you? Why?

M,I,DOUBLE S,I

How did the second longest river in the United States get its name? Mississippi may have come from an Algonquian Indian word meaning "big river."

The Rio Grande is another important river. Rio Grande is Spanish for . . . "big river"!

In Tennessee and Mississippi, you can find the Hatchie River. In the language of the local Indians, the word for *river* was *hatchie*. Later, white settlers didn't know that hatchie meant "river." So they actually called it the "river river."

It's fun to discover how places got their names! Here are some more examples.

People of the Hasinai, one of several confederacies of Caddo Indians, called each other *Tayshas*, which meant "friends" or "allies." Spanish explorers and settlers referred to the Hasinai and their homeland as *Tejas*. Later, *Tejas* became *Texas*.

Other places were named by English settlers to honor important people back in England: Yorktown for the Duke of York and Annapolis for Queen Anne.

Do you know how your home town got its name?

Cynthia in the Snow

It SUSHES.
It hushes
The loudness in the road.
It flitter-twitters,
And laughs away from me.
It laughs a lovely whiteness,
And whitely whirs away,
To be
Some otherwhere,
Still white as milk or shirts.
So beautiful it hurts.

Gwendolyn Brooks

April Rain Song

Let the rain kiss you.
Let the rain beat upon your head with silver
    liquid drops.
Let the rain sing you a lullaby.

The rain makes still pools on the sidewalk.
The rain makes running pools in the gutter.
The rain plays a little sleep-song on our roof
    at night—

And I love the rain.

Langston Hughes

BRINGING THE RAIN

A NANDI TALE
retold by Verna Aardema
illustrated by Beatriz Vidal

This is the great
   Kapiti Plain,
All fresh and green
   from the African rains—

TO KAPITI PLAIN

A sea of grass for the
   ground birds to nest in,
And patches of shade for
   wild creatures to rest in;
With acacia trees for
   giraffes to browse on,
And grass for the herdsmen
   to pasture their cows on.

But one year the rains
   were so very belated,
That all of the big wild
   creatures migrated.
Then Ki-pat helped to end
   that terrible drought—
And this story tells
   how it all came about!

This is the cloud,
    all heavy with rain,
That shadowed the ground
    on Kapiti Plain.

This is the grass,
    all brown and dead,
That needed the rain
    from the cloud overhead—
The big, black cloud,
    all heavy with rain,
That shadowed the ground
    on Kapiti Plain.

These are the cows,
    all hungry and dry,
Who mooed for the rain
    to fall from the sky;
To green-up the grass,
    all brown and dead,
That needed the rain
    from the cloud overhead—
The big, black cloud,
    all heavy with rain,
That shadowed the ground
    on Kapiti Plain.

This is Ki-pat,
  who watched his herd
As he stood on one leg,
  like the big stork bird;
Ki-pat, whose cows
  were so hungry and dry,
They mooed for the rain
  to fall from the sky;
To green-up the grass,
  all brown and dead,
That needed the rain
  from the cloud overhead—
The big, black cloud,
  all heavy with rain,
That shadowed the ground
  on Kapiti Plain.

266

This is the eagle
  who dropped a feather,
A feather that helped
  to change the weather.
It fell near Ki-pat,
  who watched his herd
As he stood on one leg,
  like the big stork bird;
Ki-pat, whose cows
  were so hungry and dry,
They mooed for the rain
  to fall from the sky;
To green-up the grass,
  all brown and dead,
That needed the rain
  from the cloud overhead—
The big, black cloud,
  all heavy with rain,
That shadowed the ground
  on Kapiti Plain.

This is the arrow
   Ki-pat put together,
With a slender stick
   and an eagle feather;
From the eagle who happened
   to drop a feather,
A feather that helped
   to change the weather.

It fell near Ki-pat,
   who watched his herd
As he stood on one leg,
   like the big stork bird;
Ki-pat, whose cows
   were so hungry and dry,
They mooed for the rain
   to fall from the sky;
To green-up the grass,
   all brown and dead,
That needed the rain
   from the cloud overhead—
The big, black cloud,
   all heavy with rain,
That shadowed the ground
   on Kapiti Plain.

This is the bow,
  so long and strong,
And strung with a string,
  a leather thong;
A bow for the arrow
  Ki-pat put together,
With a slender stick
  and an eagle feather;
From the eagle who happened
  to drop a feather,
A feather that helped
  to change the weather.

It fell near Ki-pat,
   who watched his herd
As he stood on one leg,
   like the big stork bird;
Ki-pat, whose cows
   were so hungry and dry,
They mooed for the rain
   to fall from the sky;
To green-up the grass,
   all brown and dead,
That needed the rain
   from the cloud overhead—
The big, black cloud,
   all heavy with rain,
That shadowed the ground
   on Kapiti Plain.

This was the shot
    that pierced the cloud
And loosed the rain
    with thunder LOUD!
A shot from the bow,
    so long and strong,
And strung with a string,
    a leather thong;
A bow for the arrow
    Ki-pat put together,
With a slender stick
    and an eagle feather;
From the eagle who happened
    to drop a feather,
A feather that helped
    to change the weather.

271

It fell near Ki-pat,
   who watched his herd
As he stood on one leg,
   like the big stork bird;
Ki-pat, whose cows
   were so hungry and dry,
They mooed for the rain
   to fall from the sky;
To green-up the grass,
   all brown and dead,
That needed the rain
   from the cloud overhead—
The big, black cloud,
   all heavy with rain,
That shadowed the ground
   on Kapiti Plain.

So the grass grew green,
   and the cattle fat!
And Ki-pat got a wife
   and a little Ki-pat—

Who tends the cows now,
   and shoots down the rain,
When black clouds shadow
   Kapiti Plain.

Reader's Response ∿ This poem creates beautiful
word pictures. Which one is your favorite?

MODERN RAINMAKERS

Scientists today know how to get more rain from clouds by "seeding" them with crystals of a chemical called silver iodide. Airplanes deliver the crystals to the clouds. The crystals act like seeds around which ice crystals grow. As they fall and become warmed, they become raindrops.

If you don't have silver iodide or an airplane handy, try making rain in your own kitchen. (Ask an adult to help you.)

Put a cup of water in a glass saucepan. Cover the pan with a plate filled with ice cubes. Slowly heat the water.

Droplets will form on the bottom of the plate when the warm water vapor rises and then cools as it meets the plate.

Continue to heat the water. The drops will become larger and fall back into the saucepan like raindrops from clouds falling back to earth.

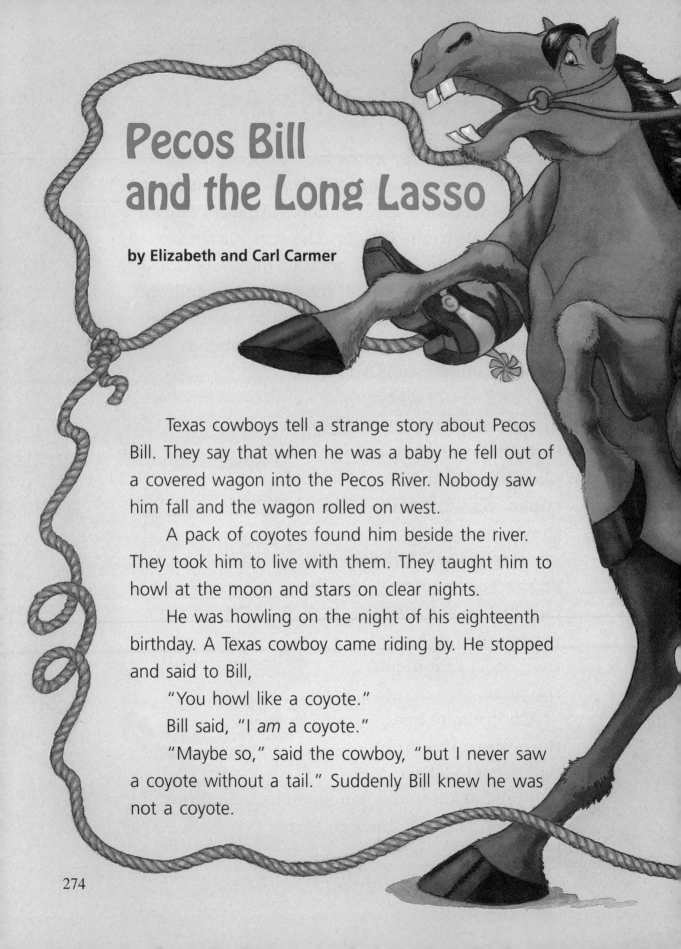

Pecos Bill and the Long Lasso

by Elizabeth and Carl Carmer

Texas cowboys tell a strange story about Pecos Bill. They say that when he was a baby he fell out of a covered wagon into the Pecos River. Nobody saw him fall and the wagon rolled on west.

A pack of coyotes found him beside the river. They took him to live with them. They taught him to howl at the moon and stars on clear nights.

He was howling on the night of his eighteenth birthday. A Texas cowboy came riding by. He stopped and said to Bill,

"You howl like a coyote."

Bill said, "I *am* a coyote."

"Maybe so," said the cowboy, "but I never saw a coyote without a tail." Suddenly Bill knew he was not a coyote.

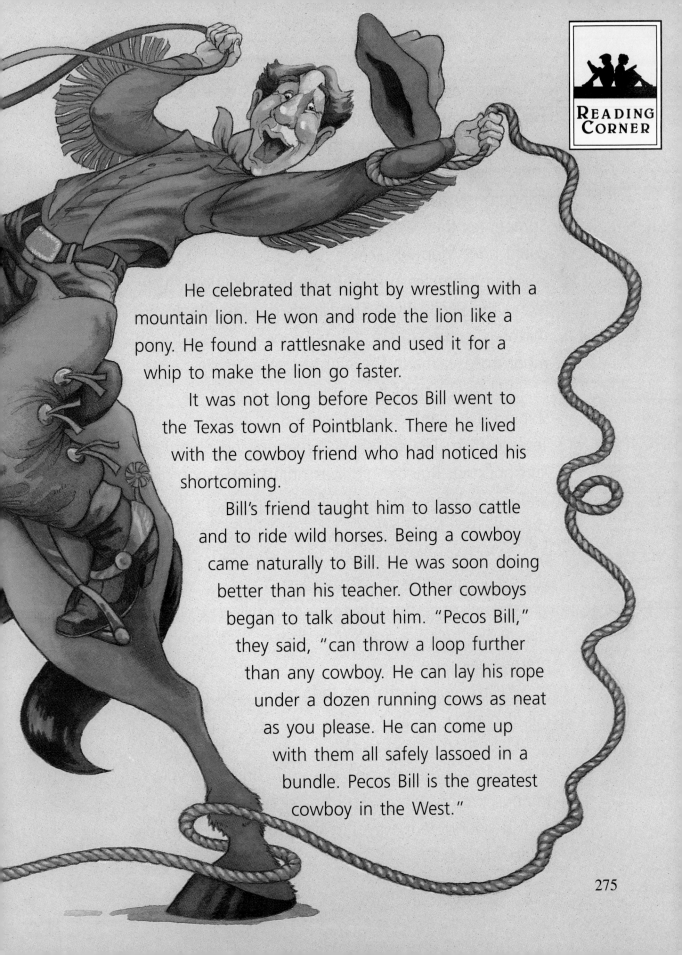

He celebrated that night by wrestling with a mountain lion. He won and rode the lion like a pony. He found a rattlesnake and used it for a whip to make the lion go faster.

It was not long before Pecos Bill went to the Texas town of Pointblank. There he lived with the cowboy friend who had noticed his shortcoming.

Bill's friend taught him to lasso cattle and to ride wild horses. Being a cowboy came naturally to Bill. He was soon doing better than his teacher. Other cowboys began to talk about him. "Pecos Bill," they said, "can throw a loop further than any cowboy. He can lay his rope under a dozen running cows as neat as you please. He can come up with them all safely lassoed in a bundle. Pecos Bill is the greatest cowboy in the West."

275

Pecos Bill broke many wild horses to the saddle. His favorite was a mustang called Widow-Maker. Other cowboys had tried to tame Widow-Maker but they failed. The horse had bucked and twisted so dangerously that they were thrown off his back. Sometimes they were badly hurt. Only Pecos Bill could ride Widow-Maker.

Late one clear night, Bill rode his Widow-Maker along the Pecos River. Thousands of stars were mirrored in the stream. Bill felt lonely. Then a round moon rose. It made the night as clear as day.

Bill saw a sight he would never forget. Down the shining river came a pretty girl riding bareback on a Texas catfish. The catfish was rearing and plunging and bucking. But the girl was riding him smoothly and easily. When she saw Bill, she edged the fish close to the river bank.

"My name is Slue-Foot Sue," she said. "I am the champion girl rider in all the west."

"You are very pretty too," said Bill.

"I like being a good rider better than being pretty," said Sue.

"Hitch your catfish to that tree," said Bill. "Let's talk it over."

"We don't need to talk it over," said Slue-Foot Sue. "I heard that no one but you could ride your famous Widow-Maker. So I boarded the nearest catfish bound your way. I'm here to prove I can ride Widow-Maker."

"But I can't let you ride him," said Bill. "You might get killed. Besides, there aren't enough pretty girls around here as it is."

"Am I pretty enough to marry?" asked Slue-Foot Sue.

"Yes, *Mam,*" said Bill.

"Then I'll tell you what I'll do," said Sue. "If you'll let me ride Widow-Maker, I'll marry you."

"That bargain isn't much good if he kills you," said Bill.

"You wouldn't lose much," said Sue. "You'd still have your horse. If you rode him around Texas you might find another pretty girl."

Bill thought and thought about it. Sue was too pretty to lose, he decided. Finally he said, "Let me talk to Widow-Maker first. Then maybe I'll let you ride him."

"That's fair enough," said Sue.

So Bill took Widow-Maker aside. "This will be the first girl who has ever tried to ride you," he said. "Don't throw her. If you don't, I'll give you an extra peck of oats every night from now until Christmas."

The horse nodded his head.

"It's all agreed," said Pecos Bill. So he lifted Slue-Foot Sue into the saddle.

At first Widow-Maker seemed to do as his master had asked. He took a few short steps to see how it felt to have a girl on his back. But Sue's skirts tickled his ribs. The tickling turned Widow-Maker into a devil. He bucked, he sprawled, he spread-eagled. He tried to throw the clinging rider from his back.

Sue held on desperately for a minute. Then she fell to the ground behind his wild hooves. Suddenly Widow-Maker doubled up like a jackknife and kicked his feet high.

Up, up went Sue into the cloudless sky. Up and up she flew until she had passed the big glowing moon. Then down she dropped on the highest slope of the India Rubber Mountain.

The mountain bounced her right back up again. Each time that she dropped onto the elastic surface, the mountain bounced her higher than before. Way down below and looking very small, stood Pecos Bill. He kept yelling to her not to be so nervous.

"I'll think of a way to bring you down," he shouted. "You'll soon be back riding your catfish in the river."

Sue had been bouncing from peak to peak all night before Pecos Bill had an idea.

He rode Widow-Maker south along the river at full gallop. In each town he borrowed everyone's lassos. The people of Dixieland gladly lent him their ropes.

He gathered all the lassos at Irabel and Crystal Water. He found even more than he expected at Red Barn.

There he stopped. He tied all the ropes together into the longest lasso in the world. Then he galloped Widow-Maker back to the India Rubber Mountain.

Now Slue-Foot Sue was still bouncing from peak to peak. Pecos Bill climbed to the mountain top. Slowly at first he began twirling the long lasso. Round his head it circled, gaining speed at every twirl. It was traveling very fast when Bill let it go. His first throw was too short. It almost got stuck on the moon. But his second throw wrapped around Sue. He pulled the lasso tight. Down she dropped into a deep valley. She swung back and forth between two mountains.

Bill pulled her up beside him. "Let's get married
this noon," he said.

"I'd like that fine," said Slue-Foot Sue.

Folks came from miles around to the big
wedding party the next week. For wedding gifts all
the guests gave Bill and Sue the lassos Bill had
borrowed.

Slue-Foot Sue and Pecos Bill lived happily for a
few months at their ranch beside the Pecos River.
But no rains came in the spring. The yellow waters
of the Pecos began to dry up. The Texas Indians
danced their rain dances. Still, not a drop of water
fell from the sky. Sue had to keep her catfish in the
old swimming hole. The rest of the river was too
shallow for him to swim in. Widow-Maker galloped
up the mountain every day. He drank the cold water
from the melting snow near the top.

One night, all the Texas stars looked as if they had been cleaned and polished.

"Bill," Sue said to her husband. "Do we still have that long lasso we got for a wedding present?"

"It's in the woodshed," said Pecos Bill.

"Please get it," said Slue-Foot Sue. "We are going to climb the mountain and I want you to bring it along."

Bill looked puzzled.

At the top of the mountain the stars looked even nearer and brighter than before.

Sue asked, "Do you see the Little Dipper?"

"Yes," said Bill.

"Can you throw our lasso over the handle?" asked Sue. "Then if we pull hard enough we might tip the dipper. The water inside would pour out."

"A good idea," shouted Bill. "I can rope it. Just give me room to get the loop started!"

Soon the lasso was circling Bill's head. It made a singing sound through the bright air. Bill kept adding more rope to its length. At last, with one great toss, Bill let it go. Up, up it went toward the stars of the Little Dipper. Sue and Bill waited. It seemed a long time before the line suddenly tightened.

"I've got it," shouted Bill. "Now pull."

Pull they did, as hard as they could. Slowly the handle of the little stardipper began to turn. Bill and Sue pulled even harder and the handle moved a little more. All night they tugged and tugged at the long rope.

Finally Sue said, "The Little Dipper's tipped enough. The water must be spilling. Let's tie the lasso fast and go home."

Daylight had begun to appear. Then suddenly there came a spatter of raindrops as big as oranges. Soon a steady stream of rain poured from the Dipper.

Bill and Sue walked home wet and happy. The falling rain washed the dusty brown trees and turned them green. The shining brown Pecos River overflowed its banks.

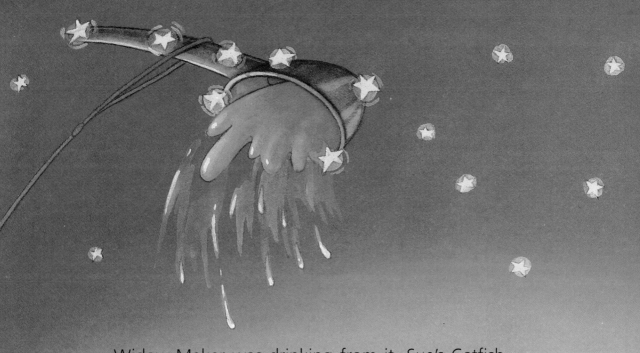

Widow-Maker was drinking from it. Sue's Catfish swam about joyfully.

Cowboys raced their mustangs through the rain drops. Indians danced outside their wigwams. The bells on their moccasins tinkled gaily.

Suddenly the rays of the rising sun struck the falling water. The biggest rainbow ever seen anywhere arched across the Texas sky.

Reader's Response ～ Which parts of this tall tale did you find the funniest?

Library Link ～ *If you enjoyed reading this tall tale, you might enjoy* Pecos Bill Rides a Tornado, *retold by Wyatt Blassingame.*

BROWSING FOR BOOKS

And on This Shelf We Have . . .

By now you have probably discovered that libraries are very much like supermarkets. In the supermarket each kind of food has its own special section. When you know just where to find cereals or ice cream or fruit juices, it's easy, and fun, to go looking for your favorite kind.

In the library, different kinds of books also have their own special sections. You probably wouldn't have any trouble going right to the table that has those large picture books you liked before you could read. By now you have probably found some other kinds of books and can even picture where you went to get them. There was that book about caring for cats that you needed when someone gave you a new kitten. Or there was the mystery story that your friend said you should read.

Your library has many kinds of books, and they are waiting for you to discover them. Reading a book of fairy tales might be a wonderful way to spend part of the weekend. Or, you might like a book about a real person, like Abraham Lincoln, Martin Luther King, Jr., Amelia Earhart, or Babe Ruth. Those are only some of the many kinds of books you'll find by browsing in your library. Take an hour to browse. It could be the best hour you'll spend all week.

The Wreck of the
Zephyr

written and illustrated by
CHRIS VAN ALLSBURG

Once, while traveling along the seashore, I stopped at a small fishing village. After eating lunch, I decided to take a walk. I followed a path out of the village, uphill to some cliffs high above the sea. At the edge of these cliffs was a most unusual sight—the wreck of a small sailboat.

An old man was sitting among the broken timbers, smoking a pipe. He seemed to be reading my mind when he said, "Odd, isn't it?"

"Yes," I answered. "How did it get here?"

"Waves carried it up during a storm."

"Really?" I said. "It doesn't seem the waves could ever get that high."

The old man smiled. "Well, there is another story." He invited me to have a seat and listen to his strange tale.

"In our village, years ago," he said, "there was a boy who could sail a boat better than any man in the harbor. He could find a breeze over the flattest sea. When dark clouds kept other boats at anchor, the boy would sail out, ready to prove to the villagers, to the sea itself, how great a sailor he was.

''One morning, under an ominous sky, he prepared to take his boat, the *Zephyr*, out to sea. A fisherman warned the boy to stay in port. Already a strong wind was blowing. 'I'm not afraid,' the boy said, 'because I'm the greatest sailor there is.' The fisherman pointed to a sea gull gliding overhead. 'There's the only sailor who can go out on a day like this.' The boy just laughed as he hoisted his sails into a blustery wind.

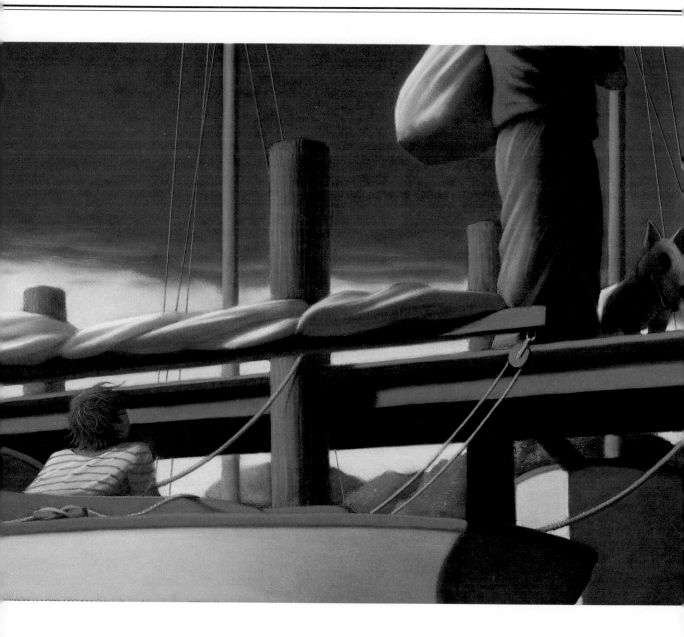

"The wind whistled in the rigging as the *Zephyr* pounded her way through the water. The sky grew black and the waves rose up like mountains. The boy struggled to keep his boat from going over. Suddenly a gust of wind caught the sail. The boom swung around and hit the boy's head. He fell to the cockpit floor and did not move.

"When the boy opened his eyes, he found himself lying on a beach. The *Zephyr* rested behind him, carried there by the storm. The boat was far from the water's edge. The tide would not carry it back to sea. The boy set out to look for help.

"He walked for a long time and was surprised that he didn't recognize the shoreline. He climbed a hill, expecting to see something familiar, but what he saw instead was a strange and unbelievable sight. Before him were two boats, sailing high above the water. Astonished, he watched them glide by. Then a third sailed past, towing the *Zephyr*. The boats entered a bay that was bordered by a large village. There they left the *Zephyr*.

"The boy made his way down to the harbor, to the dock where his boat was tied. He met a sailor who smiled when he saw the boy. Pointing to the *Zephyr* he asked, 'Yours?' The boy nodded. The sailor said they almost never saw strangers on their island. It was surrounded by a treacherous reef. The *Zephyr* must have been carried over the reef by the storm. He told the boy that, later, they would take him and the *Zephyr* back over the reef. But the boy said he would not leave until he learned to sail above the waves. The sailor told him it took years to learn to sail like that. 'Besides,' he said, 'the *Zephyr* does not have the right sails.' The boy insisted. He pleaded with the sailor.

"Finally the sailor said he would try to teach him if the boy promised to leave the next morning. The boy agreed. The sailor went to a shed and got a new set of sails.

"All afternoon they sailed back and forth across the bay. Sometimes the sailor took the tiller, and the boat would magically begin to lift out of the water. But when the boy tried, he could not catch the wind that made boats fly.

"When the sun went down they went back to the harbor. They dropped anchor and a fisherman rowed them to shore. 'In the morning,' the sailor said, 'we'll put your own sails back on the *Zephyr* and send you home.' He took the boy to his house, and the sailor's wife fed them oyster stew.

"After dinner the sailor played the concertina. He sang a song about a man named Samuel Blue, who, long ago, tried to sail his boat over land and crashed:

For the wind o'er land's ne'er steady nor true,
an' all men that sail there'll meet Samuel Blue.

"When he was done with his song, the sailor sent the boy to bed. But the boy could not sleep. He knew he could fly his boat if he had another chance. He waited until the sailor and his wife were asleep, then he quietly dressed and went to the harbor. As he rowed out to the *Zephyr*, the boy felt the light evening wind grow stronger and colder.

"Under a full moon, he sailed the *Zephyr* into the bay. He tried to remember everything the sailor had told him. He tried to feel the wind pulling his boat forward, lifting it up. Then, suddenly, the boy felt the *Zephyr* begin to shake. The sound of the water rushing past the hull grew louder. The air filled with spray as the boat sliced through the waves. The bow slowly began to lift. Higher and higher the *Zephyr* rose out of the water, then finally broke free. The sound of rushing water stopped. There was only the sound of wind in the sails. The *Zephyr* was flying.

"Using the stars to guide him, the boy set a course for home. The wind blew very hard, churning the sea below. But that did not matter to the *Zephyr* as she glided through the night sky. When clouds blocked the boy's view of the stars, he trimmed the sails and climbed higher. Surely the men of the island never dared fly so high. Now the boy was certain he was truly the greatest sailor of all.

"He steered well. Before the night was over, he saw the moonlit spire of the church at the edge of his village. As he drew closer to land, an idea took hold of him. He would sail over the village and ring the *Zephyr*'s bell. Then everyone would see him and know that he was the greatest sailor. He flew over the tree-topped cliffs of the shore, but as he reached the church the *Zephyr* began to fall.

"The wind had shifted. The boy pulled as hard as he could on the tiller, but it did no good. The wind shifted again. He steered for the open sea, but the trees at the cliff's edge stood between him and the water. At first there was just the rustle of leaves brushing the hull. Then the air was filled with the sound of breaking branches and ripping sails. The boat fell to the ground. And here she sits today."

"A remarkable tale," I said, as the old man stopped to relight his pipe. "What happened to the boy?"

"He broke his leg that night. Of course, no one believed his story about flying boats. It was easier for them to believe that he was lost in the storm and thrown up here by the waves." The old man laughed.

"No sir, the boy never amounted to much. People thought he was crazy. He just took odd jobs around the harbor. Most of the time he was out sailing, searching for that island and a new set of sails."

A light breeze blew through the trees. The old man looked up. "Wind coming," he said. "I've got some sailing to do." He picked up a cane, and I watched as he limped slowly toward the harbor.

GLOSSARY

Full pronunciation key* The pronunciation of each word is shown just after the word, in this way: **abbreviate** (ə brē′vē āt).

The letters and signs used are pronounced as in the words below.

The mark ′ is placed after a syllable with a primary or heavy accent as in the example above.

The mark ′ after a syllable shows a secondary or lighter accent, as in **abbreviation** (ə brē′vē ā′shən).

SYMBOL	KEY WORDS	SYMBOL	KEY WORDS	SYMBOL	KEY WORDS
a	ask, fat	u	up, cut	r	red, dear
ā	ape, date	ʉr	fur, fern	s	sell, pass
ä	car, father			t	top, hat
		ə	a in ago	v	vat, have
e	elf, ten		e in agent	w	will, always
er	berry, care		e in father	y	yet, yard
ē	even, meet		i in unity	z	zebra, haze
			o in collect		
i	is, hit		u in focus	ch	chin, arch
ir	mirror, here			ŋ	ring, singer
ī	ice, fire	b	bed, dub	sh	she, dash
		d	did, had	th	thin, truth
o	lot, pond	f	fall, off	*th*	then, father
ō	open, go	g	get, dog	zh	s in pleasure
ô	law, horn	h	he, ahead		
oi	oil, point	j	joy, jump	′	as in (ā′b′l)
oo	look, pull	k	kill, bake		
o͞o	ooze, tool	l	let, ball		
yo͞o	unite, cure	m	met, trim		
yo͞o	cute, few	n	not, ton		
ou	out, crowd	p	put, tap		

*Pronunciation key and respellings adapted from *Webster's New World Dictionary, Basic School Edition*, Copyright © 1983 by Simon & Schuster, Inc. Reprinted by permission.

A

ab·bre·vi·a·tion (ə brē′ vē ā′ shən) *noun.* a shortened form of a word or phrase.

a·ca·cia tree (ə kā′shə trē′) *noun.* a tall shrub that grows in warm parts of the world. It has feathery leaves and bunches of yellow or white flowers. **acacia trees.**

ad·mire (əd mīr′) *verb.* to think of someone or something with approval and respect: Everyone *admired* the painting at the museum. **admired.**

ad·vis·er or **ad·vis·or** (əd vīz′ər) *noun.* a person who gives ideas to others, often used by leaders of countries or businesses to help solve problems. **advisers, advisors.**

a·larm (ə lärm′) *noun.* **1.** a warning of danger given by shouting, ringing bells, etc. **2.** a sudden call to fight. **3.** fear caused by danger.

a·lert (ə lʉrt′) *verb.* to warn people to be ready for possible danger.

an·e·mom·e·ter (an′ə mom′ə tər) *noun.* an instrument used to measure how fast the wind blows.

an·i·mal groom·er (an′ə m′l grōōm′ər) *noun.* a person who is paid to take special care of animals, such as brushing hair, clipping nails, etc.: The *animal groomer* carefully cut the poodle's hair.

an·nals (an″lz) *plural noun.* **1.** records of important things written down year by year in the order they happened. **2.** historical records.

anx·ious·ly (aṉgk′shəs lē) *adverb.* **1.** in an uneasy or worried way. **2.** wishing eagerly.

as·sign (ə sīn′) *verb.* **1.** to give out a task or job: The teacher *assigned* us a book report. **2.** to set aside for a special reason or purpose. **assigned.**

as·sist·ant (ə sis′tənt) *noun.* someone who assists or helps another person; helper.

acacia tree

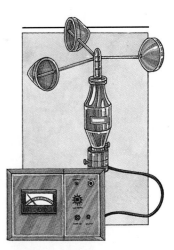

anemometer

atlas

Atlas was the name given to a book of maps because such books often had a picture of Atlas, the Greek god who held the world on his shoulders.

bamboo

baobab

at·las (at′ləs) *noun.* a book of maps.

at·mos·phere (at′məs fir) *noun.* **1.** all the air around the earth: The earth's *atmosphere* is made up of different gases. **2.** the air in a place. **3.** the general feeling or mood of a place or thing.

at·tach (ə tach′) *verb.* **1.** to fasten or join together as by tying or sticking; to connect. **2.** to bring close by feelings of love. **3.** to add to the end of something.

a·ward (ə wôrd′) *noun.* a prize given for excellence or in recognition of some achievement. **awards.**

B

bam·boo (bam boo′) *noun.* tall grass that grows like a tree in hot, or tropical, regions of the world. The hollow, woody stems are used in making window blinds, canes, fishing poles, and other things. **bamboos.**

ban·dage (ban′dij) *noun.* a strip or piece of cloth used to cover a sore, cut, or wound.

ba·o·bab (bā′ō bab′) *noun.* a tree with a wide trunk that grows in parts of Africa and India. **baobabs.**

barge (bärj) *noun.* a large boat with a flat bottom, used to carry heavy things on rivers and canals: The *barge* stopped at many places along the river to pick up different kinds of goods.

ba·ton (bə ton′) *noun.* **1.** a thin stick used by the leader of an orchestra, band, or chorus to direct the group. **2.** a large stick twirled by a drum major or majorette.

beast (bēst) *noun.* any large animal that has four feet: The campers were awakened by a *beast* searching for food.

be·fall (bi fôl′) *verb.* to happen to or come to pass: Sometimes, bad luck *befalls* us all. **befalls.**

be·lat·ed (bi lāt′id) *adjective.* too late; not on time: He sent a *belated* birthday card to his friend.

bi·cus·pid (bī kus′pid) *noun.* a tooth with two points on top.

bind (bīnd) *verb.* **1.** to tie together with rope or cloth; to tie tightly. **2.** to wrap a bandage around something. **3.** to keep together because of strong feelings or beliefs.

bird of par·a·dise (bʉrd uv par′ə dīs) *noun.* **1.** any of a number of brightly colored birds from New Guinea. **2.** a plant from Africa with large, pointed flowers resembling a bird's beak.

blimp (blimp) *noun.* a lighter-than-air airship shaped like an egg, used to carry people or things.

blot (blot) *verb.* **1.** to make spots on; stain. **2.** to block or hide: We *blotted* out our tracks in the dirt so we would not be followed. **3.** to soak up liquid using paper, sponges, etc. **blotted.**

boast (bōst) *verb.* to talk about what you have or what you have done with too much pride; to brag: We were tired of the way he *boasted* about winning the medal. **boasted.**

both·er (bo*th*′er) *verb.* **1.** to cause trouble or worry; annoy: We were *bothered* by all the noise in the gym. **2.** to take the time to do something. **bothered.**

bought (bôt) *verb. the past tense and past participle of* **buy.** to have received something by paying money for it: He *bought* the game at the toy store.

bridge (brij) *noun.* **1.** the thin, curved piece of a violin over which strings are stretched. **2.** something built across a river, railroad tracks, etc., so that people or cars can cross over. **3.** the upper, bony part of the human nose. **4.** a platform above the main deck of a ship, from which the ship is controlled.

bris·tle (bris″l) *verb.* to stand up stiffly like thick hair. **bristling.**

brit·tle (brit″l) *adjective.* easily broken because it is hard and stiff.

browse (brouz) *verb.* **1.** to nibble at leaves, twigs, or grass: Giraffes often *browse* in tall trees. **2.** to look through a book, stopping to read different parts. **3.** to look over things for sale.

a fat	oi oil	ch chin
ā ape	oo look	sh she
ä car, father	o͞o tool	th thin
e ten	ou out	*th* then
er care	u up	zh leisure
ē even	ur fur	n̄g ring
i hit		
ir here	ə = a *in* ago	
ī bite, fire	e *in* agent	
o lot	i *in* unity	
ō go	o *in* collect	
ô law, horn	u *in* focus	

————————◇————————

Blimp got its name from a type of aircraft called a *limp*. Limps were soft unless they were filled with the gas that made them lighter than air. There were two types of limps: A and B. The B limp was the most common. Soon its name was changed to blimp.

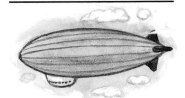

blimp

315

C

calculator

cal·a·bash (kal′ə bash) *noun.* **1.** a tree found in tropical areas, having a fruit that looks like a gourd. **2.** a bowl or other container made of the dried, hollow shell of a gourdlike fruit.

cal·cu·la·tor (kal′kyə lāt′ər) *noun.* a machine that does arithmetic quickly.

car·pen·ter (kär′pən tər) *noun.* a person who builds or repairs things made of wood. **carpenter's.**

cat·a·logue *or* **cat·a·log** (kat″l ôg) *noun.* **1.** a printed list or book with pictures and descriptions of things for sale: We looked through several *catalogues,* but we could not find the boots we wanted. **2.** a file of cards in alphabetical order that is a complete list of things, such as all the books in a library. **catalogues** *or* **catalogs.**

ceil·om·e·ter (sē lom′ə tər) *noun.* an instrument that measures the height of clouds above the ground.

chant (chant) *verb.* to talk in a sing-song way, sometimes over and over. —*noun.* a song with many words sung in the same tone.

char·ac·ter (kar′ik tər) *noun.* **1.** someone in a story or play. **2.** a person's thoughts, feelings, and actions; what a person is like. **3.** any letter, or symbol that is used in writing or printing, or in a computer. **characters.**

cher·ish (cher′ish) *verb.* to treat someone or something with love and care; take care of; treasure. **cherishes.**

chief (chēf) *noun.* the leader of a group: We took our orders from the *chief.* —*adjective.* **1.** in the highest position. **2.** first in size; most important.

chor·tle (chôr′t′l) *verb.* to laugh; to make a gleeful chuckle. **chortled.**

chuck·le (chuk″l) *verb.* to laugh softly. **chuckled.**

churn (churn) *verb.* **1.** to move or stir around with great force: The wind *churned* the leaves around the field. **2.** to beat cream until it turns to butter. **churned.**

clar·i·net (klar ə net′) *noun.* a musical instrument played by blowing in a mouthpiece while covering the holes with fingertips or with keys.

cla·vier (klə vir′) *noun.* any instrument having strings and a keyboard, such as the piano or harpsichord.

cloak (klōk) *noun.* **1.** a loose piece of outer clothing, usually having no sleeves. **2.** something that covers or hides.

coax (kōks) *verb.* to repeatedly ask someone to do something. **coaxed.**

cock·a·too (kok′ə tōō) *noun.* a parrot with a crest on its head and white feathers colored in places with pink and yellow. **cockatoos.**

col·o·nist (kol′ə nist) *noun.* a person who, with others, settles in another land, far from his or her home country: Early *colonists* from Europe were helped by the Native Americans in North America. **colonists.**

com·pose (kəm pōz′) *verb.* **1.** to write or create, especially music: He *composed* a beautiful song. **2.** to make by mixing two or more things together. **composed.**

com·pos·er (kəm pō′zər) *noun.* a person who composes, especially one who writes music.

con·cert (kon′sərt) *noun.* a program of music in which musicians play together.

con·duc·tor (kən duk′tər) *noun.* **1.** a person who directs an orchestra: Everyone applauded when the *conductor* came on stage. **2.** the person who collects tickets or money on a train.

con·ser·va·to·ry (kən sur′və tor′ē) *noun.* **1.** a room, enclosed in glass, for growing and showing plants; a small greenhouse. **2.** a school of music, art, etc.

con·stant (kon′stənt) *adjective.* **1.** always the same; unchanging. **2.** loyal or faithful.

con·test (kon′test) *noun.* **1.** a race, game, etc., in which each person or team tries to win. **2.** a struggle or fight.

cour·ti·er (kôr′tē ər) *noun.* a person present at a royal palace or court; an attendant. **courtiers.**

a fat	oi oil	ch chin
ā ape	oo look	sh she
ä car, father	oo tool	th thin
e ten	ou out	*th* then
er care	u up	zh leisure
ē even	ur fur	ŋ ring
i hit		
ir here	ə = a *in* ago	
ī bite, fire	e *in* agent	
o lot	i *in* unity	
ō go	o *in* collect	
ô law, horn	u *in* focus	

cockatoo

Cockatoo comes from Malaysia, a country in the South Pacific. There, they call this type of noisy parrot *kakatuwa*, or "old big sister."

creeper

cre·ate (krē āt') *verb.* **1.** to make something for the first time: We watched as the artist *created* a beautiful statue. **2.** to cause or make happen. **created, creating.**

creep·er (krēp'ər) *noun.* **1.** any plant that grows along the ground or a wall and whose stem puts out threadlike parts that hold it in place. **2.** a person or thing that moves along with the body close to the ground.

cure (kyoor) *verb.* to make a sick person well; to return to good health: The doctor *cured* my sore throat. **cured.**

delicate

D

de·fense·less (di fens'lis) *adjective.* being helpless; not able to protect oneself.

del·i·cate (del'i kit) *adjective.* **1.** slight and not easily felt: The child used a *delicate* touch when she picked up the flowers. **2.** light, mild, or soft; not strong. **3.** very finely made. **4.** easily broken.

del·i·ca·tes·sen (del'i kə tes"n) *noun.* a store that sells foods that are ready to eat, such as cheeses, cooked meats, etc.

de·light·ful (di līt'fəl) *adjective.* very pleasing; giving great pleasure or delight.

den·tine (den'tēn) *noun.* the hard, bony material forming the main part of the tooth.

de·scend·ant (di sen'dənt) *noun.* a person who is related by birth to someone, or some family, who lived many years before. **descendants.**

des·o·late (des'ə lit) *adjective.* **1.** lonely; unhappy; miserable. **2.** not lived in; abandoned.

dig·ni·ty (dig'nə tē) *noun.* **1.** pride or self-respect: She accepted the award with great *dignity*. **2.** the condition of being worthy of respect.

dis·may (dis mā') *noun.* **1.** alarm or shock; great fear. **2.** a loss of courage when faced with a problem or danger.

drought (drout) *noun.* a long period of time when there is little or no rain. **droughts.**

E

earn (urn) *verb*. **1.** to be paid for work that is done: She *earns* money for walking her neighbor's dog. **2.** to get or deserve because of something you have done. **earns.**

e·mo·tion·al·ly (i mō′shən′l ē) *adverb*. in a way that shows strong or deep feelings.

en·tire (in tīr′) *adjective*. having no missing parts; complete or whole.

es·say (es′ā) *noun*. a short written piece giving the author's opinions about some subject.

e·val·u·ate (i val′yoo wāt) *verb*. **1.** to use information to make a judgment. **2.** to find out what something is worth. **evaluating.**

e·ven·tu·al·ly (i ven′choo wəl ē) *adverb*. finally; in the end: All the leaves *eventually* fell from the tree.

ex·act (ig zakt′) *adjective*. **1.** correct to the smallest detail: My *exact* height is 5 feet, 5¼ inches. **2.** having no mistakes.

ex·pe·ri·ence (ik spir′ē əns) *noun*. **1.** anything that has happened to a person: Getting lost in the forest and seeing a bear were frightening *experiences*. **2.** skill that is gained through training and practice. **experiences.**

ex·plo·sion (ik splō′zhən) *noun*. **1.** an outburst, especially of noise or color: The *explosion* of fireworks was beautiful to watch. **2.** a fast or sudden increase in something.

ex·pres·sion (ik spresh′ən) *noun*. **1.** a look that shows what one feels or means. **2.** the act of putting something into words. **3.** a certain way of speaking, reading, singing, etc., that is persuasive, graceful, gives meaning, etc. **4.** a common word or saying. **expressions.**

ex·traor·di·nar·y (ik strôr′d'n er′ē) *adjective*. very different from what is usual; remarkable; very unusual.

a fat	**oi** oil	**ch** chin
ā ape	**oo** look	**sh** she
ä car, father	**o͞o** tool	**th** thin
e ten	**ou** out	**th** then
er care	**u** up	**zh** leisure
ē even	**ur** fur	**ṅg** ring
i hit		
ir here	ə = a *in* ago	
ī bite, fire	e *in* agent	
o lot	i *in* unity	
ō go	o *in* collect	
ô law, horn	u *in* focus	

explosion

Extraordinary is made up of two words, *extra* and *ordinary*. Sometimes *extra* means "more than usual." In this case, *extra* means "on the outside." So *extraordinary* means "something outside of the ordinary" or "something very special."

figurehead

F

fig·ure·head (fig′yər hed) *noun.* **1.** a carved wooden figure placed on the front of a ship for decoration. **2.** a person who seems important but who has no real power.

flam·boy·ant (flam boi′ənt) *adjective.* **1.** very colorful and fancy. **2.** too showy or fancy. *noun.* a tropical tree with showy red and orange flowers; also called *royal poinciana.*

flaw·less (flô′les) *adjective.* without a blemish; perfect.

flute (flōot) *noun.* a musical wind instrument. It is played by blowing across a mouthpiece while covering different holes with fingers.

flute

fore·cast (fôr′kast) *verb.* to tell or try to tell what will happen ahead of time; predict: The weather reporter has *forecast* rain for this afternoon.

for·mu·la (fôr′myə lə) *noun.* a set of directions for mixing a medicine, baby's food, etc.

fran·gi·pa·ni (fran′jə pan′ē) *noun.* a tropical shrub with large, fragrant flowers.

frangipani

fu·ri·ous (fyoor′ē əs) *adjective.* full of anger or rage: He was *furious* when his bicycle was broken.

G

gasp (gasp) *verb.* to take a sudden breath because of surprise, shock, or some other strong feeling. **gasped.**

gen·er·a·tion (jen′ə rā′shən) *noun.* a group of people who are all born and live around the same time and who often have many of the same kinds of experiences: People of his parents' *generation* used to dance to rock 'n' roll music.

gnarled (närld) *adjective.* twisted and knotty.

gong (gông) *noun.* a round, metal plate that makes a loud, deep ringing sound when struck with a stick.

good·ie bag (good′ē bag) *noun.* a sack that holds useful things, such as items to help tell a story, or gifts to be handed out.

gown (goun) *noun.* **1.** a long, loose piece of clothing, such as a woman's long dress, usually worn at special times. **2.** a long, loose robe worn by a minister, judge, etc. **gowns.**

gro·cer·ies (grō′sər ēz) *plural noun.* goods such as food and household supplies.

320

gust (gust) *noun.* a strong, sudden rush of air: A *gust* of wind blew off his hat.

H

ham·let (ham′lit) *noun.* a very small village. **hamlets.**

ham·mock (ham′ək) *noun.* a long piece of net or canvas that is hung between two trees and used as a bed or couch.

har·mo·ny (här′mə nē) *noun.*
1. a pleasing arrangement of parts, things, etc.: The flowers in the vase were a *harmony* of colors.
2. musical sounds of different tones played or sung together in a pleasing way.

her·ald (her′əld) *noun.* a person who announces important news.

herds·man (hʉrdz′mən) *noun.* a person who watches over a herd, or group, of animals. **herdsmen.**

hol·low (hol′ō) *adjective.* having an empty space or a hole inside; not solid: The *hollow* log was used to make a canoe.

hoof·beat (hoof′bēt′ *or* hoof′bēt′) *noun.* sound made by any hoofed animal such as a horse when it runs or walks: The villagers heard *hoofbeats* in the distance. **hoofbeats.**

hor·net (hôr′nit) *noun.* a large wasp that lives in a nest and can give a painful sting. **hornets.**

hu·mid·i·ty (hyoo mid′ə tē) *noun.* the amount of water in the air; dampness.

hur·ri·cane (hʉr′ə kān) *noun.* a powerful storm with heavy rain and winds that blow in a circle at 73 or more miles per hour.

hy·grom·e·ter (hī grom′ə tər) *noun.* an instrument used to measure humidity.

I

i·mag·i·na·tion
(i maj′ə nā′shən) *noun.*
1. the ability to picture things in the mind. **2.** the ability to make up things that are not real or did not really happen.

a fat	ɔi oil	ch chin
ā ape	oo look	sh she
ä car, father	oo tool	th thin
e ten	ou out	*th* then
er care	u up	zh leisure
ē even	ur fur	ng ring
i hit		
ir here	ə = a *in* ago	
ī bite, fire	e *in* agent	
o lot	i *in* unity	
ō go	o *in* collect	
ô law, horn	u *in* focus	

Hamlet is a very old word that has gone through many changes. It is based on the Old English word for *home*.

Hurricane was an old Spanish word that meant "an evil spirit from the sea."

hygrometer

instructor

ivory

im·pe·ri·al (im pir′ē əl) *adjective.* having to do with an empire, emperor, or empress; royal.

im·press (im pres′) *verb.* to affect strongly a person's ideas or feelings about someone or something: We were all *impressed* by his report. **impressed.**

in·de·pend·ence (in′di pen′dəns) *noun.* the condition of freedom from being controlled by others: The thirteen American colonies declared their *independence* from England in 1776.

in·flu·ence (in′floo wəns) *noun.* the power or ability to affect persons or things: He used his *influence* to get us tickets for the basketball playoffs.

in·form (in fôrm′) *verb.* to tell about or give facts about something: She was *informed* that the train would arrive late. **informed.**

in·struct·or (in struk′tər) *noun.* a teacher or someone who teaches.

in·stru·ment (in′strə mənt) *noun.* **1.** a device used for making musical sounds: The piano is my favorite *instrument.* **2.** a tool used for a certain kind of work.

in·tel·li·gence (in tel′ə jəns) *noun.* the ability to learn, think, and understand.

in·ter·rupt (in tə rupt′) *verb.* **1.** to break into or upon something, such as someone talking; stop for a while. **2.** to get in the way of; to cut off. **interrupted.**

isle (īl) *noun.* an island, usually a small island.

i·vo·ry (ī′vər ē) *adjective.* **1.** made of the hard white substance that forms the tusks of elephants, walruses, etc. **2.** creamy-white in color: Over the years, the *ivory* color of the piano keys turned yellow with age.

J

jas·mine (jaz′min) *noun.* a tropical plant with fragrant white, red, or yellow flowers, one type of which is used to make perfume.

L

lane (lān) *noun.* **1.** a narrow path or road between hedges, walls, or buildings. **2.** a path for ships, cars, airplanes, etc., that are going in the same direction, as in a highway with four lanes. **lanes.**

leop·ard (lep′ərd) *noun.* a large, wild animal of the cat family, found in Africa and Asia. *Leopards* usually have a tan coat with black spots. **leopards.**

lev·ee (lev′ē) *noun.* **1.** a bank or pile of earth built along a river to keep it from overflowing: The people built *levees* to protect their homes from the flood. **2.** a place for ships to dock along a river. **levees.**

li·brar·i·an (lī brer′ē ən) *noun.* a person trained to work in a library.

lu·pine (lōō′pin) *noun.* a garden plant with tall, white, pink, yellow, or blue flowers and pods with beanlike seeds. **lupines.**

M

mel·o·dy (mel′ə dē) *noun.* musical tones arranged to make a tune or song, often the main part of a piece of music.

mem·o·ry (mem′ər ē) *noun.* **1.** the power of storing facts, ideas, names, etc., in the mind and recalling them as needed. **2.** all that can be remembered. **3.** a thought of someone or something from the past. **4.** the amount of information a computer can store or the parts of a computer that store information.

men·u (men′yōō) *noun.* **1.** the particular foods chosen for each course of a meal. **2.** a list of foods and drinks that can be ordered at a restaurant. **3.** a list of programs on a computer or a list of choices in a computer program.

a fat	oi oil	ch chin
ā ape	oo look	sh she
ä car, father	ōō tool	th thin
e ten	ou out	th then
er care	u up	zh leisure
ē even	ur fur	ŋ ring
i hit		
ir here	ə = a *in* ago	
ī bite, fire	e *in* agent	
o lot	i *in* unity	
ō go	o *in* collect	
ô law, horn	u *in* focus	

Leopard has two parts, *leo* and *pard*. *Leo* means "lion," and *pard* means "spotted."

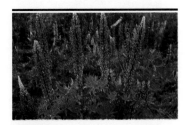

lupine

323

mother-of-pearl

Nickname is a word that developed from a common mistake. The word *eke* used to mean "also" or "added." An *ekename* meant an "extra name." Over the years people began to say *nekename*. Finally, it changed to *nickname*.

noble

me·te·or·ol·o·gist (met′ē ə rol′ə jist) *noun.* a scientist who studies the weather.

mi·grate (mī′grāt) *verb.* **1.** to move from one country or place and settle in another. **2.** to move to a different place each season, as some animals do. **migrated.**

mi·nor (mi′nər) *adjective.* **1.** of lesser size, importance, amount, etc. **2.** in music, a tone that is one-half step from the next tone instead of one full step.

mois·ture (mois′chər) *noun.* water or other liquid that causes a slight wetness or dampness in the air.

moo (mo͞o) *verb.* to make the sound a cow makes. **mooed.**

moth·er-of-pearl (mu*th*′ər əv purl′) *adjective.* made of the hard, pearly inside layer of certain seashells.

mourn (môrn) *verb.* to feel or show sorrow or grief over a loss, someone's death, etc. **mourned.**

mur·mur (mur′mər) *verb.* **1.** to make a low, steady sound. **2.** to speak in a very low voice. **murmured.**

N

nick·name (nik′nām) *noun.* name often used instead of the real name of a person, place, or thing, given in fun or out of strong liking: The tall boy's *nickname* is Stretch.

no·ble (nō′b′l) *noun.* a person who has a high rank or royal title. **nobles.**

nov·el (nov″l) *noun.* a long story, usually a book, about imaginary characters and events.

nu·mer·i·cal (no͞o mer′i k′l *or* nyo͞o mer′i k′l) *adjective.* **1.** shown as a number instead of a letter. **2.** of or having to do with a number or numbers.

O

ob·ject (ob′jikt) *noun.* a thing that can be seen or touched; something that has shape and takes up space. **objects.**

odds (odz) *plural noun.* a difference that makes one thing more likely to happen than another.

or·ches·tra (ôr′kis trə) *noun.* a group of people who play musical instruments together, usually in public.

or·di·nar·y (ôr′d'n er′ē) *adjective.* not special; normal; usual.

or·gan (ôr′gən) *noun.* **1.** a musical instrument with keys, pedals, and pipes of different sizes. Air is forced through the pipes to make different tones. **2.** a certain part of the body such as the heart or lungs.

P

palm (päm) *noun.* any of a number of trees, found in warm parts of the world, with large leaves at the top of a tall, branchless trunk.

pas·ture (pas′chər) *verb.* **1.** to feed on growing grass. **2.** to put animals out to feed on growing grass: The farmers *pasture* their sheep on the meadows by the river. —*noun.* a grassy area where sheep, cattle, and other animals can graze.

pa·tient (pā′shənt) *noun.* a person who is being treated by a doctor or dentist: Each of the *patients* waited her turn to see the doctor. **patients.**

peas·ant (pez″nt) *noun.* a farm worker or farmer of a small farm, as in Europe or Asia. **peasants.**

per·suade (pər swād′) *verb.* to get someone to act or think a certain way by making it seem like a good idea. **persuaded.**

pet·al (pet″l) *noun.* one of the colorful leaves of a plant that forms the flower. **petals.**

phrase (frāz) *noun.* **1.** two or more words that give a single idea or mean something, but are not a complete sentence. **2.** a short passage of music, usually of two, four, or eigh measures. **phrases.**

pierce (pirs) *verb.* **1.** to mak a hole in. **2.** to go through or into. **pierced.**

a fat	ơi oil	ch chin
ā ape	ơơ look	sh she
ä car, father	ōō tool	th thin
e ten	ơu out	*th* then
er care	u up	zh leisure
ē even	ur fur	nĝ ring
i hit		
ir here	ə = a *in* ago	
ī bite, fire	e *in* agent	
o lot	i *in* unity	
ō go	o *in* collect	
ô law, horn	u *in* focus	

orchestra

organ pipes

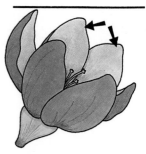

petals

possum

plow·horse (plou'hôrs') *noun.* a horse used to pull a farming tool that turns over the soil before seeds are planted. **plowhorses.**

pop·u·lar (pop'yə lər) *adjective.* **1.** liked by many people. **2.** very well liked by one's own friends. **3.** believed by many people, as in: a *popular* idea.

po·si·tion (pə zish'ən) *noun.* **1.** the usual or proper way a person or thing is placed. **2.** the place where a person or thing is, especially how near or far from other things. **3.** a job that someone has. **positions.**

pos·sum (pos'əm) *noun.* *a shorter form of* **opossum.** a small American animal that lives in trees, carries its young in a pouch, and plays dead when it is in danger.

prai·rie (prer'ē) *noun.* a large, level or rolling area of land covered with grass and having few trees: The wagons crossed the *prairie* in the hot, August sun.

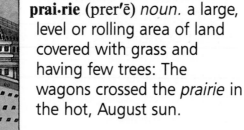

prow

pre·cious (presh'əs) *adjective.* **1.** very valuable; expensive: Our rivers and forests are *precious* resources. **2.** much loved; cherished. **3.** overly delicate or refined; unnatural.

price (prīs) *noun.* the amount of money that is asked or given for something: The *price* of the dress I want to buy is $25.00.

prince (prins) *noun.* **1.** the son or grandson of a king, queen, or other royal ruler. **2.** a ruler whose rank is below that of a king.

pro·fes·sion·al (prə fesh'ən'l) *adjective.* **1.** of or about a person who earns a living at something that needs special learning or training: The tailor is proud of his *professional* skill. **2.** working in a particular job for pay, as a professional writer.

pro·test (prə test') *verb.* to speak strongly against something; to disagree or object. **protested.**

prow (prou) *noun.* the front or forward part of a boat or ship. **prows.**

326

Q

quar·ter-size (kwôr′tər sīz′) *adjective.* equal to ¼ of the usual size.

quench (kwench) *verb.* **1.** to put out, as a fire. **2.** to satisfy or lessen: A cool glass of water will *quench* her thirst.

R

ra·dar (rā′där) *noun.* a device that sends out and picks up radio waves that bounce off faraway objects. The radio waves are then used to locate objects.

ra·di·o·sonde (rā′dē ō sond′) *noun.* an instrument sent up by balloon and used to measure the temperature, humidity, and air pressure of the upper atmosphere.

re·al·ize (rē′ə līz) *verb.* **1.** to understand completely: I *realized* that my report would require a lot of time to prepare. **2.** to make real; bring into being; achieve. **realized.**

Red·coat (red′kōt) *noun.* a British soldier at the time when they wore red coats, as at the time of the American Revolution. **Redcoats.**

re·flect (ri flekt′) *verb.* **1.** to give back an image, as a mirror or water does: The setting sun was *reflected* in the lake. **2.** to bend or throw back, as light, heat, sound, etc. **reflected.**

reg·i·ment (rej′ə mənt) *noun.* a group of soldiers who fight together as a unit.

re·hears·al (ri hur′səl) *noun.* time spent practicing in order to prepare for a performance.

rein (rān) *verb.* to guide, slow, or stop a horse by pulling long leather straps connected to each side of the metal bar in the horse's mouth. **reined.**

res·cue (res′kyoo) *verb.* to free or save from danger or harm: The lifeguard *rescued* the swimmer from drowning. **rescued.**

rose-col·ored (rōz′kul′ərd) *adjective.* **1.** pinkish- or purplish-red in color. **2.** bright, cheerful, or hopeful.

a fat	oi oil	ch chin
ā ape	oo look	sh she
ä car, father	oo tool	th thin
e ten	ou out	th then
er care	u up	zh leisure
ē even	ur fur	ŋ ring
i hit		
ir here	ə = a *in* ago	
ī bite, fire	e *in* agent	
o lot	i *in* unity	
ō go	o *in* collect	
ô law, horn	u *in* focus	

radar

Radar is made up of the first letters of the words in the phrase *Radio Detecting and Ranging,* which is the longer name of the radar device.

RSVP has almost become a word in English, but it is not really a word. The letters are the first letters of four French words, *respondez s'il vous plait*. In French, the words mean "respond if you please." In modern English, RSVP is a polite way of asking someone to answer the invitation.

rough (ruf) *adjective*. **1.** not smooth or level: The car rocked back and forth as it moved along the *rough* road. **2.** having bumps or projections; uneven. **3.** not gentle or careful.

roy·al (roi′əl) *adjective*. **1.** fit for a king or queen; magnificent; splendid. **2.** of, from, or by a king or queen. **3.** of a kingdom, its government, etc.

RSVP *or* **r.s.v.p.** *phrase*. initials of the French phrase meaning "please reply."

ru·in (rōō′in) *verb*. **1.** to damage or destroy. **2.** to make poor. **ruined.**

S

sa·cred (sā′krid) *adjective*. **1.** pertaining to religion, or set aside for a religious purpose; holy. **2.** given or deserving great respect; hallowed: The burial ground was *sacred* to them. **3.** that must be kept or not ignored, as a *sacred* promise.

scroll (skrōl) *noun*. **1.** a roll of paper or parchment with writing or pictures on it. **2.** a decoration in the form of a scroll.

scroll

scur·ry (skᵘr′ē) *verb*. run quickly: When the cat pounced, the mouse *scurried* under the couch. **scurried.**

se·lec·tion (sə lek′shən) *noun*. **1.** a thing or things chosen. **2.** a choosing or being chosen. **3.** things from which to choose.

shrug (shrug) *verb*. to draw the shoulders up toward the head to show that one does not care or does not know. **shrugged.**

skin·ner (skin′nər) *noun*. **1.** an old term for a person who steals or cheats. **2.** someone who strips animal skins or prepares them for sale. **skinners.**

slaugh·ter (slôt′ər) *noun*. **1.** the slaying of animals for food; butchering. **2.** the killing of people in a cruel way or in large numbers, as in a bloody battle. —*verb*. **1.** to kill for food; butcher. **2.** to kill people or animals cruelly or in large numbers: Because buffalo were *slaughtered* in such large numbers, they almost became extinct. **slaughtered.**

slen·der (slen′dər) *adjective*. **1.** long and thin: James is *slender* even though he eats a lot. **2.** small in size or amount.

slope (slōp) *noun.* **1.** land that is not flat; slanted like a hillside. **2.** a surface, line, etc., that slants.

sock·et (sok′it) *noun.* a hollow part into which something fits or which holds something: Carefully screw the light bulb into the *socket.*

so·lo·ist (sō′lō ist) *noun.* a performer who sings, dances, etc., alone on stage, or a person who does something alone.

splot (splot) *noun. shortened form of* **splotch.** an uneven spot, splash, or stain.

stamp (stamp) *verb.* **1.** to bring or put the foot down hard. **2.** to put a postage stamp on a letter or package to be mailed.

steam sho·vel (stēm′ shuv″l) *noun.* a large, mechanically operated digger powered by steam. **steam shovels.**

stur·dy (stur′ dē) *adjective.* strongly built; made to last a long time.

sub·way (sub′wā) *noun.* an underground railroad on which people travel from one place to another in some large cities.

swirl (swurl) *verb.* to move by twisting or spinning around and around: The wind *swirls* snow over the fields. **swirling.**

T

tech·nol·o·gy (tek nol′ə jē) *noun.* the use of scientific ideas to invent tools to solve everyday problems.

thick·et (thik′it) *noun.* an area where bushes, plants, and small trees grow thickly: The *thicket* was so dense we could not walk through it and had to find another way to the brook.

thong (thôn͡g) *noun.* a narrow strip of leather used as a lace, strap, etc.

thorn (thôrn) *noun.* a short, sharp point that grows on the stems of some plants such as rose bushes: Be careful not to prick your finger on the *thorns.* **thorns.**

tor·na·do (tôr nā′dō) *noun.* a tall, thin column of air that moves very fast and destroys things in its path. **tornados** or **tornadoes.**

a fat	ɔi oil	ch chin
ā ape	oo look	sh she
ä car, father	ōō tool	th thin
e ten	ou out	*th* then
er care	u up	zh leisure
ē even	ur fur	n͡g ring
i hit		
ir here	ə = a *in* ago	
ī bite, fire	e *in* agent	
o lot	i *in* unity	
ō go	o *in* collect	
ô law, horn	u *in* focus	

slope

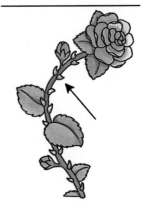

rose **thorns**

treasure chest

trumpet

tract (trakt) *noun.* **1.** a large area of land, water, desert, etc.: The settlers built their farms on large *tracts* of land. **2.** a number of organs in the body working together to carry out some function, for example, the digestive *tract* . **tracts.**

treas·ure (trezh′ər) *noun.* **1.** a collection of valuable things such as money, gold, etc. **2.** a person or thing that is greatly loved.

tre·men·dous (tri men′dəs) *adjective.* **1.** very large or huge. **2.** wonderful; marvelous.

trom·bone (trom bōn′ *or* trom′bōn) *noun.* a brass musical instrument with a long, bent tube that slides in and out to change the sound it makes.

trop·i·cal (trop′i k′l) *adjective.* of, in, or about the very hot climates of the earth, near the equator.

trudge (truj) *verb.* to walk slowly, as if very tired: We saw John *trudging* up the hill after he jogged two miles. **trudging.**

trum·pet (trum′pit) *noun.* a brass instrument with a long, looped tube that ends in a funnellike opening.

type (tīp) *verb.* to write with a typewriter; to use such a machine to produce printed words.

U

un·u·su·al (un yōō′zhōō wəl) *adjective.* not common, usual, or ordinary; rare: It's *unusual* to have such warm weather in February.

V

val·u·a·ble (val′yōō b′l *or* val′yōō wə b′l) *adjective.* **1.** worth a lot of money. **2.** thought of as important or very useful.

ver·sion (vʉr′zhən) *noun.* a story told from one point of view; a different form of something: People who saw the accident told the police different *versions* of who caused it. **versions.**

vi·o·la (vē ō'lə) *noun.* a stringed musical instrument that is like a violin, but larger and with a deeper tone.

vi·o·lin (vī ə lin') *noun.* a musical instrument with four strings, played with a bow.

vi·o·lin·ist (vī ə lin'ist) *noun.* a person who plays the violin.

vol·un·teer (vol'ən tir') *verb.* to do something out of choice, of one's own free will. **volunteered.**

vow (vou) *verb.* **1.** to make a solemn promise. **2.** to say in a forceful or earnest way. **vowed.**

W

---

wharf (hwôrf) *noun.* a long platform built from the shore out over the water, so that ships can easily discharge passengers and unload cargo. **wharves.**

whirl·ing (hwurl'ing) *adjective.* quickly spinning around and around.

whoosh (hwo͞osh *or* wo͞osh) *verb.* to move with a loud hissing sound. **whooshed.**

winch (winch) *noun.* a machine that uses a chain or rope to pull or lift things.

wis·dom (wiz'dəm) *noun.* the quality of intelligence and good judgment that tells one what to do and what is right or wrong.

word pro·ces·sor (wurd pros'es sôr) *noun.* a computer used to write, edit, and store letters and records.

work·shop (wurk'shäp) *noun.* **1.** a place where work is done. **2.** a meeting where a group of people study, talk, or work on special projects: Our teacher went to three *workshops* to learn about new ways to use classroom materials. **workshops.**

a fat	oi oil	ch chin
ā ape	o͞o look	sh she
ä car, father	o͞o tool	th thin
e ten	ou out	th then
er care	u up	zh leisure
ē even	ur fur	ng ring
i hit		
ir here	ə = a *in* ago	
ī bite, fire	e *in* agent	
o lot	i *in* unity	
ō go	o *in* collect	
ô law, horn	u *in* focus	

violin

wharf

ABOUT THE
Authors & *Illustrators*

VERNA AARDEMA

▲ Verna Aardema began writing stories because her little girl liked to listen to a story while she was eating. "She could make a scrambled egg last all the way through 'Little Red Riding Hood.' After a time I began to make up little feeding stories. That way she didn't know how far off the end would be." Later, Verna Aardema began writing and publishing the stories she told to her daughter. *(Born 1911)*

GARY APPLE

■ Gary Apple writes plays, funny stories, and scripts for television. He believes that young writers should not be afraid to put their ideas on paper. He says, "If you think of a poem or a story or a play or just an idea you like, write it down. Don't worry if it's good or bad, just put it on paper. You can go back later and change what you have written, but first you have to have the ideas on paper. Your creative thoughts are wonderful things. Writing is a way to save those thoughts forever."

GWENDOLYN BROOKS

✳ The poet Gwendolyn Brooks was born in Topeka, Kansas. She says, "I loved poetry very early and began to put rhymes together at about seven." At the age of thirteen her poem "Eventide" was accepted and printed in a children's magazine. When she was sixteen she began submitting poems to a newspaper, and more than 75 of them were published. Gwendolyn Brooks won the Pulitzer Prize in poetry in 1950 for *Annie Allen*. *(Born 1917)*

DROLLENE P. BROWN

▲ Drollene P. Brown grew up in West Virginia and now lives in Florida. Her book *Sybil Rides for Independence* is about a real person who lived more than 200 years ago. Ms. Brown wrote another book about a real person who lived about 100 years ago. That book told the story of Belva Lockwood, a woman who ran for president in 1884. Ms. Brown enjoys writing about interesting people who lived long ago. She also enjoys meeting young readers and talking to them. *(Born 1940)*

CARL CARMER

Many of the books Carl Carmer wrote were illustrated by his wife, Elizabeth Black Carmer. He and his wife also wrote some books together. Carl Carmer said that as a child, he was "fascinated by the sound and color of words." He thought that books for young people should be simple but well-written. "I take my writings for kids just as seriously as for adults." *(1893–1976)*

ELIZABETH CARMER

Elizabeth Carmer grew up in New Orleans. She said she enjoyed drawing from the time she was a little girl. "With the first crayons and chalks came the desire to paint." After she married Carl Carmer, she moved to New York. She and her husband wrote books together. She also illustrated some of the books he wrote. *(1904–1982)*

MARY BLOUNT CHRISTIAN

▲ Mary Blount Christian was born in Houston, Texas. She is married and has three children. All her life she has been interested in writing. She says: "As an only child, I told stories to myself and my imaginary playmates, rewrote fairy tales into plays to present to the neighborhood children, and wrote stories (mostly scary ones) on every scrap of paper." She has written a number of books and is working on writing more. *(Born 1933)*

MARCHETTE CHUTE

■ Marchette Chute writes both poetry and nonfiction books. Many of her books are written because she gets curious about something. She says, "I set out to find everything I can about it." She enjoys looking things up, even when the research takes a long time. "The research and writing," she says, "is sometimes very slow. . . . But I never fail to enjoy myself, just as I never fail to start my next book with the same sense of delighted curiosity about what I will find." *(Born 1909)*

BEVERLY CLEARY

* Beverly Cleary says that she had a hard time learning to read when she was young. After she learned to read, she wondered why there weren't books about plain, ordinary boys and girls. "Why couldn't authors write about the sort of boys and girls who lived on my block?" She decided that when she grew up she would write books about ordinary people. Beverly Cleary has won many awards, including the Newbery Medal. *(Born 1916)*

BARBARA COONEY

▲ Barbara Cooney writes and illustrates her books for young people. She also illustrates books by other authors. She won the Caldecott Medal for *Chanticleer and the Fox*. This story was first told by Geoffrey Chaucer, an English poet who lived in the 1300s. Barbara Cooney retold Chaucer's story and illustrated it with beautiful drawings. *(Born 1917)*

LINDA GOSS

Linda Goss loves to tell stories. Some of the stories she tells are new stories. Some of them are old. She tells stories she has heard from other people, and she makes up her own stories, too. When Linda Goss tells stories, she doesn't use just her voice. She also uses her hands, her face, pieces of cloth, and jewelry. Before she starts a story, she rings bells to tell people to gather around her because the story is about to begin. Linda Goss is the "Official Storyteller of Philadelphia."

GAIL E. HALEY

Gail E. Haley writes and illustrates books for young people. She has won many awards, including the Kate Greenaway Medal and the Caldecott Medal. She says many people ask her what it's like to be a Caldecott winner. "They might as well ask: 'What is it like to become Miss America, a Nobel Laureate, or a winner of the Irish Sweepstakes?' Any of these are wildly happy surprises—frosting on the cake of life." *(Born 1939)*

MARGARET HILLERT

Margaret Hillert writes poems and stories. She also taught school. "In my poetry and stories," she says, "I write about things I like myself: *cats,* Teddy bears, biking, *cats,* colored leaves, *cats,* etc. . . . One of my cats usually sits on my chest and 'helps'—or sits on my lap at the typewriter." Margaret Hillert has been writing poems since she was in the third grade. *(Born 1920)*

EFNER TUDOR HOLMES

Efner Tudor Holmes was born in Boston, Massachusetts. She is married and has two children. She says that she writes about animals and country living because she likes both these things. She is also interested in farming, music, and travel. Her mother, Tasha Tudor, is a well-known illustrator of children's books. *(Born 1949)*

LEE BENNETT HOPKINS

✸ Lee Bennett Hopkins has interviewed, or talked with, many writers and illustrators. He writes about his talks with these people. He also writes poems for young people. He says, "I love doing children's books. Each one is a new challenge, a new day, a new spring for me." Lee Bennett Hopkins also puts together anthologies, or collections, of other people's poems. He goes through thousands of poems and chooses the twenty that he thinks children will enjoy most. *(Born 1938)*

LANGSTON HUGHES

▲ Langston Hughes said he began to write poetry because he was elected Class Poet when he was in grammar school. He said, "The day I was elected, I went home and wondered what I should write. Since we had eight teachers in our school, I thought there should be one verse for each teacher, with an especially good one for my favorite teacher." When he grew up, he wrote many poems. He also wrote stories and novels. Langston Hughes won many awards for his writing. *(1902–1967)*

JOHANNA HURWITZ

■ Johanna Hurwitz is a writer and illustrator of books for young people. She is also a children's librarian. She says, "My parents met in a bookstore, and there has never been a moment when books were not important in my life. . . . I loved the library so much that I made the firm decision by age ten that someday I would become a librarian." At the same time, she planned that she would write books, too. Johanna Hurwitz says she likes to write letters to friends and relatives. "I am sure the letter writing that I do has been the best type of training for my book writing." *(Born 1937)*

SUSAN JEFFERS

✳ Susan Jeffers has always liked to draw. She remembers that when she was young she decorated her skis, paper book covers—even her rain slicker— with colorful paintings. Her art career began when she created a historical mural for her class in school. Today she is an internationally admired illustrator, filling her books with unforgettable images of nature, fairy tale characters, and classic heroes and heroines.

JEANETTE LEARDI

▲ Jeanette Leardi is a writer and an editor. She writes articles for *Child Life* and *Sesame Street Magazine* and also writes poetry. She wanted to be a writer since she was in the sixth grade, when she helped to start a school newspaper. She says, "I believe that there are two things that anyone who wants to be a writer must do: read a lot and write a lot." She also believes that it is important to write about something you care about, and adds, "Don't get discouraged if you don't write exactly what you want to say. With practice all writers become better writers." *(Born 1952)*

ARNOLD LOBEL

■ Arnold Lobel wrote and illustrated books for children. Many of his books have won awards. *Frog and Toad Are Friends* was a Caldecott Honor Book, and *Frog and Toad Together* was a Newbery Honor Book. Arnold Lobel enjoyed creating books for children. He once said, "There is a little world at the end of my pencil. I am the stage director, the costume designer, and the man who pulls the curtain. When a character is not behaving as I would wish him to, he can be quickly dismissed with a wave of my eraser." *(1933–1987)*

MISKA MILES

Miska Miles's real name was Patricia Miles Martin. She wrote many stories and poems for children. Her book *The Gods in Winter* was an IBBY honor book. She said she began writing when she was a young child visiting her grandfather's farm in Kansas. "At Grandfather's, I used to go up into the barn loft. . . . The barn was always partly full of hay, and the smell was dusty and sweet. I remember sitting in the big open doorway listening to the rain on the roof, smelling the sweet country fragrance, a lined tablet on my lap, describing the things I saw and smelled and heard." *(1899–1986)*

MOTHER GOOSE

Mother Goose may or may not have been a real person. Some people say she was. Some people say she was not. The name *Mother Goose* was first used in France more than three hundred years ago. In the early 1700s, in Boston, there was a woman named Elizabeth Goose. She sang rhymes to her seven small grandchildren. The children's father is said to have collected the rhymes and verses, but the book has never been found. Even if that woman was Mother Goose, she did not make up the rhymes she sang. Many of them are known to be three or four hundred years old. A few of them are said to be even older.

EVALINE NESS

Evaline Ness wrote books for children. She also illustrated her own books and the books of other authors. She said that it was hard to illustrate her own books. She thought that her books should be published with blank spaces for readers to draw their own pictures. The publishers did not agree with her. She won many awards, including the Caldecott Medal for *Sam, Bangs & Moonshine.* Several of her books were also Caldecott Honor Books and American Library Association Notable Books. *(1911–1986)*

MICHELLE NIKLY

Michelle Nikly lives in Europe. When she wrote *The Emperor's Plum Tree,* she wrote it in French. The story was published in France. Then someone decided that it would be a good story for children in the United States to read. So the story was retold in English.

343

DANIEL MANUS PINKWATER

▲ Daniel Manus Pinkwater writes and illustrates books for young people. He enjoyed reading when he was growing up. He says Mark Twain is his favorite author. After he graduated from college, he worked for several years as a sculptor. When Daniel Manus Pinkwater began writing books, he was more interested in the illustrations than the writing. He says, "Writing was a bit of a challenge. . . . Then the stories became more interesting to me." Some of Daniel Manus Pinkwater's books have been American Library Association Notable Books and Junior Literary Guild selections. *(Born 1941)*

CHARLES M. SCHULZ

■ Charles M. Schulz is the man who created the comic strip *Peanuts.* He says that Snoopy, the dog in *Peanuts,* was modeled after a dog he had when he was growing up. His dog was called Spike. Charles Schulz says, "I had decided that the dog in the strip was to be named 'Sniffy,' until one day, just before the strip was actually published, I was walking past a newsstand and glanced down at the rows of comic magazines. There I saw one about a dog named Sniffy, so I had to think of another name. Fortunately, before I even got home, I recalled my mother once saying that if we ever had another dog, we should name him 'Snoopy.' " That is how Snoopy got his name. *(Born 1922)*

ELIZABETH SHUB

▲ Elizabeth Shub was born in Poland. She came to the United States when she was a child. She writes books for children. Her book *The White Stallion* was an American Library Association Notable Book. She also translates books into English. She helped Isaac Bashevis Singer translate *Zlateh the Goat and Other Stories* from Yiddish.

WILLIAM STEIG

■ William Steig writes and illustrates books for young people. He did not begin writing for children until he was sixty years old. Before that, he drew cartoons for magazines. Now, he has won many awards for his books for young people. He won the Caldecott Medal for *Sylvester and the Magic Pebble*. He once said, "Winning is definitely fun. I never understood what was missing from my life until this began to happen. It feels darn good." *(Born 1907)*

CHRIS VAN ALLSBURG

❋ Chris Van Allsburg is an author and illustrator. He has won many awards for his work. He received the Caldecott Medal for *Jumanjii*. Some of his other books have been Caldecott Honor Books, American Library Association Notable Books, and Boston Globe—Horn Book honor books. He began creating children's books when his wife started teaching school. She would bring books home from school and tell him that he, too, could write good books. Chris Van Allsburg says he enjoys getting letters from people who have read his books. *(Born 1949)*

DIANE WOLKSTEIN

▲ Diane Wolkstein lives in New York City. Some of her children's books have been chosen as American Library Association Notable Books. Diane Wolkstein is also a storyteller. She teaches storytelling to teachers and librarians. She has made records of stories from different lands and has traveled to Europe to tell her stories. *(Born 1942)*

ED YOUNG

Ed Young was born in Tientsin, China, the son of Qua-Ling and Yuen Teng Young. He attended City College of San Francisco and the University of Illinois and did graduate study at Pratt Institute. He is the illustrator of a number of books and has received many awards. He received the Caldecott Medal and the Boston Globe Horn Book Award for *Lon Po Po: A Chinese Red Riding Hood Tale.* Ed Young also teaches a Chinese exercise called Tai Chi Chuan. He says "Tai Chi Chuan is beneficial to mind and body; the whole of the person. This exercise has had profound influence upon my way of thinking and on the things that I do." *(Born 1931)*

AUTHOR INDEX

Allsburg; 313, Deirdre Griffin; 314, Claudia Sargent, Deirdre Griffin; 315, Barbara Lanza; 316, Melinda Fabian; 318, Deirdre Griffin; 319 Barbara Lanza; 320, Melinda Fabian; 321, Claudia Sargent; 325, Deirdre Griffin; 326, Claudia Sargent; 328, Diane Dawson Hearn; 329, Roberta Holmes, Deirdre Griffin; 330, Barbara Lanza; 331, Claudia Sargent; 168-174, Tamar Haber-Schaim.

PHOTOGRAPHY: 12-13, SuperStock; 13, Mimi Forsyth/Monkmeyer Press; 15, Ken O'Donoghue; 21, The Bettmann Archive; 32, Brent Petersen; 35, Walter H. Scott; 37, Evelyn Flaret, PEOPLE WEEKLY,© Time Inc.; 39, Ken Heyman/Black Star; 56, 59, Rick Browne; 61, The American Library Association; 80-81, Dan McCoy/Rainbow; 81, JUNGLE TALES (CONTES DE LA JUNGLE), oil on canvas, by James Jebusa Shannon, American, 1895, 34 1/4" x 44 3/4", Arthur Hoppock Hearn Fund, 1913, 13.143.1,© The Metropolitan Museum of Art, New York; 82-83; Ken Kauffman; 142-143, Patricia J. Bruno/Positive Images; 143, HAVING A BALL, Multi-media sculpture by George Rhoads, American, 1984, photo by Wayne Sorce; 144, Ken O'Donoghue; 198, 201, The Granger Collection; 203-204, Erich Lessing/Magnum; 228-229, Sonya Jacobs/ The Stock Market; 229, UMBRELLAS IN THE RAIN, painting by Maurice Prendergast, 1899, American, 1859-1924, watercolor, 14" x 20 7/8" (355 x 530 mm), Charles Henry Hayden Fund, Museum of Fine Arts, Boston; 239, Peter Menzel; 240-248, Glenn Oakley; 249, Robert Campbell/Index Stock International; 317, Ruth Lacey; 318, Stephen G. Maka; 320, (t) Ruth Lacey, (b) Frank Siteman; 322, (t) Richard Pasley/Stock, Boston, (b) Ira Kirschenbaum/Stock, Boston; 323, Tom Pantages; 324, (b) The Bettmann Archive; 325, (t) Milton Feinberg/Stock, Boston, (b) George Malave/Stock, Boston; 326, Larry West/Bruce Coleman; 331, Gale Zucker/Stock, Boston; 332, (t) Los Angeles Times; 333, Los Angeles Times; 335, (t) Macmillan Publishing Company, (b) The Bettmann Archive; 336, (b) courtesy, Penguin USA; 337, (t) Ken Kauffman, (b) By Studio Cole Ltd., courtesy, Macmillan Publishing Company; 339, (t) provided by author; 340, (t) Viking Penguin, (b) courtesy, Penguin USA; 341, (t) Viking Penguin; 342, (t) Little, Brown and Company, (b) The Bettmann Archive; 343, courtesy, Clift Hotel/Henry Holt & Company; 344, (t) Victoria Beller-Smith, (b) courtesy, United Feature Syndicate; 345, (t) H.W. Wilson Company, (b) Anne Hall; 346, (t) courtesy, Houghton Mifflin Co., (b) H.W. Wilson Company; 347, courtesy, Putnam Publishing Group.